May 2022

TO CAL STATE SAN BERNARDINO

Exce
"Ever L
Get Sober and Stay Sober
Go to Bed Sober, Wake up Sober
Art Gilles

D0821358

KINd REGUARdS

Art Gilles

(ALUMNi)

A.K.A. (DONALD GILLESPIE

SOBRIETY CASTLE

The Fall and Rise of Stuart MacPherson

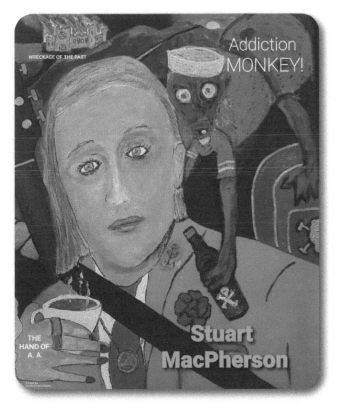

WRECKAGE OF THE PAST

Addiction
MONKEY!

THE
HAND OF
A. A.

Stuart
MacPherson

Alcoholism is a lonely demon.

A Novel by
ART GILLES

(This book is illustrated.)

PAGE PUBLISHING
Conneaut Lake, PA

First originally published by Page Publishing 2021

Original artwork paintings by Donald Stuart Gillespie

Sobriety Castle is a *fictional novel.* The names, characters, locations, organizations, and incidents are derived from the imagination of the author *or* are used *fictitiously.*

Any resemblance to actual events, locales, or persons either living or dead is entirely coincidental.

ISBN 978-1-6624-3782-3 (pbk)
ISBN 978-1-6624-3472-3 (hc)
ISBN 978-1-6624-3471-6 (digital)

Printed in the United States of America

CONTENTS

**Sobriety Castle
The Fall and Rise
of Stuart MacPherson
A novel by Art Gilles
"Alcoholism is a lonely demon."**

What this book is about!

Sobriety Castle
The Fall and Rise of Stuart MacPherson
A novel by Art Gilles
"Alcoholism is a lonely demon."

Sobriety Castle is a must-read "dramedy" self-help novel for understanding alcoholism and other addictive behaviors with exciting and entertaining stories of romance and adventure.

Year 1963: Young US Navy sailor Stuart is a Polaris missile crane cab operator aboard USS *Hunley (AS-31)* in HolyLoch, Scotland where one night he befriends **the wandering ghost of Queen Anne**. Join the fictional character Stuart MacPherson on his international roller-coaster ride from the bottomless pit of oblivion from using alcohol and other drugs to a world of hope and success through recovery.

Learn how alcoholism affects families and, in our story, how Stuart's faithful and courageous wife, Maria, stood by her husband through the worst of times and later, once Stuart became sober, through the best of times.

Once in recovery, Stuart fights his demons daily and soon learns that in order to stay clean and sober himself, he must dedicate his life to helping others, who are the suffering, near-dead alcoholics and addicts—who have no clue that there is a way out of addiction. To that end, Stuart founded a sober living home called **Sobriety Castle**.

ACKNOWLEDGMENTS

Thanks to all caring individuals who are in recovery and are helping others to be free of the bondage of addictions and to those sober living homes, recovery units, and treatment centers that are truly motivated, altruistically and not for money, to help reach out to seemingly helpless and hopeless alcoholics to help them find a better life—*sober.*

And to those who encouraged me to write this book—Steve, Alex, Alicia, Mabel, Caroline, Kim, Ronald and Kimberly, Allison, and Leigh-Ann.

Thanks for being my friend, Wayne. And kudos to all 12-step programs out there! Thanks also to Elliott and Lana for helping me with the publishing of this book.

It's Easier to
STAY SOBER
than to
GET SOBER !

Artwork by:
Donald Stuart Gillespie

CHAPTER ONE

Burning Desire

The sun is going down over the mountains of San Bernardino. A train whistle is heard in the distance. A Bentley car is driving down the 215 Freeway. A lady's hand turns on the radio to select her music. The song she plays is called "Rehab" by Amy Winehouse. Someone is riding a Harley motorcycle on a country section of Route 66, passing a Route 66 sign. It is dusk.

A big rig truck drives up to the right side of a white ranch fence and parks. The white fence is around what looks like the entrance to a little village. The Bentley drives into the entrance. Park-style lamps surround the driveway into the village. A gazebo is on the right. A swan fountain is by the first building. The Bentley parks. More cars are coming in—a pickup truck (all beat up). Some guy that looks homeless rides in on a bicycle. The motorcycle rider drives in. A guy on the motorcycle gets off, has tons of keys. He goes up to the door of the first cottage-like house and opens the door to a meeting room.

The guy from the truck starts making coffee. A well-dressed lady is carrying a tray of cookies. A car full of ladies arrive. One is in sexy attire, and the others look beat up. A van with twelve guys arrive (from a rehab center).

Tables and chairs are being set up in the meeting room. There is the sound and smell of coffee brewing. People are spread now both inside and in front of the meeting room, which appears to have a magical quality to it.

Everyone is chatting with one another using first names only. Both men and women greet one another with a hug. It is indeed an odd-looking group of people gathered from all walks of life—people totally different from one another, who would never, under normal conditions, mix.

Candles are being placed around the table. All the people are sitting around the table. The candles are lighted.

Suddenly, all the lights go out, and it's dark, except for the candlelight. The noisy room becomes totally silent.

A voice announces: "My name is Stuart... and I'm an alcoholic. Welcome to the *Burning Desire Candlelight Meeting!*"

Outside, suddenly it gets windy, very dark, and thunder and lightning flashes behind silhouetted trees. The blue outline of a woman's face appears high up in the dark clouds above Sobriety Castle.

CHAPTER TWO

NOW IT BEGINS

(As Told to Me by Stuart MacPherson Himself)

1945

Born in Camden, New Jersey, then lived in a small town nearby, I was only three years old and already began to wander about alone unattended.

I walked alone around the corner and was brought home by a policeman. At four, I got stung by bees at a church parking lot and scared to death by a bulldog and by other kids. Also at four years old, both parents worked, and I got used to being alone. I had a sister three years older than myself. We did not talk much. I also had a brother who was seventeen years older and was away in the Army Air Force. I still have a photo of me at three years old up on his shoulders while he was in his military uniform.

Now I was in a new town—Plainfield, New Jersey—and I was five years old. My grandfather was about seventy-five years old and was an active Methodist minister. My grandmother was ninety years old. We were all living in a large elegant three-story home. It still had gaslight fixtures on the walls of the rooms, oak floors, and even an old-fashioned hand water pump in the large backyard. A two-story garage was located at the end of a circular driveway. Beautiful yard. Grandfather planted a garden and a vineyard. Soon my grandparents would move out to be near grandfather's new church.

I was in a nice middle-class house but lonely. Already at five years old, I was restless, irritable, and discontented. I was a latchkey kid, left alone because all the adults disappear while working during the day until 4:30 p.m.

Both of my parents and grandparents and my older brother graduated from prestigious colleges. And my great grandfather was a US Consul, appointed by three different presidents, and he represented the United States in three different countries.

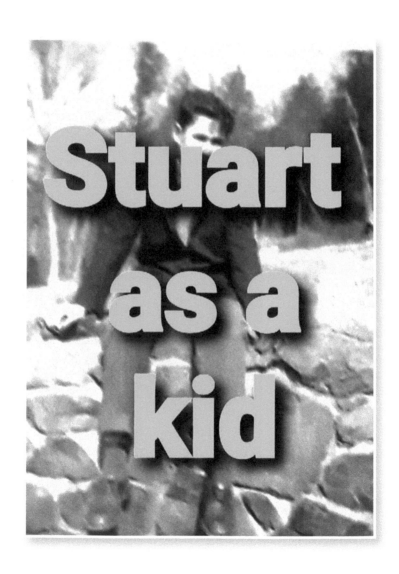

U.S. Consul to BORNEO
Orlando Harrison Baker
1911 Appointment by
U.S. President
Theodore Roosevelt

At age sixty, in the year 1896, my great-grandfather was appointed as the US Consul to Denmark by US president Benjamin Harrison. In the year 1900, he was appointed as US Consul to Australia by US President William McKinley. Then, in 1908, a final appointment as US Consul in Borneo was made by President Theodore Roosevelt. My great-grandfather was returning to the US on vacation at eighty years old. But his ship got quarantined in Japan, and everyone on it died.

I inherited his possessions, which included a top hat and a real headhunter's sword carved out of human bone with hair with a large engraved designs on metal blade. But it was nice to have surprise gifts. Now after this, I was really feeling different and alone. I looked at the headhunter's sword. It scared me.

Even at five years old, I felt like I really needed a drink. There were two things in life I had discovered. What really happened around me and to me as a child—I didn't really know—and then there in my mind's eye was what I thought happened to me as a child. Two different things. The drama in the lives of the adults around me went on like an endless soap opera.

My mother had a master's degree from Columbia University and worked first as a social worker then as a probation officer for the county. My dad worked for the state as an employment appeals officer. After work, he would relax with a glass of booze—namely, Port Sherry. Then, his personality would transform instantly.

I would hide in my room, and my mother saved me. My mom was overly protective of me, and she did not drink.

I was often spanked with a board and often verbally abused by my father. Once at six, I got some wood and was in the process of building a great rocket ship using a hammer, nails, and orange crates. It was coming along very nicely. But now, my father came home, had his drink, and then came and saw my rocket ship. Instead of saying, "Wow, that looks great," like I had hoped for, my father got angry and smashed my rocket ship to pieces and told me it would never fly and that also I would never grow up to amount to anything. But I wanted to learn how to play music.

So I was still six years old, going to first grade. A girl in my class lived a few blocks away from my house. She said her cat had some kittens.

"Can I come over to look at them?"

I remembered the house smelled funny, and they had something I had never seen before: a tin of pretzels. So while I was enjoying pretzels and something else new, ginger ale, she brought out a box of kittens. I picked out a gray kitten. It was winter, and when I petted the kitten, it made sparks. So I took it home without asking my parents first. Thankfully, they let me keep the cat. I named it Sparky. At last, I had a friend—a gray cat.

One day my parents were arguing about something. My father was drunk. I was afraid, so I decided to run away from home. It was about 4:30 p.m.

Down at the end of my tree-lined street was a quarter-mile grand entrance to a very large public park. So that was where I was headed to. I'd planned to sleep in the bushes near the park lake. Little did I realize, two homeless alcoholic bums were already in those bushes.

So I finally completed the tree-lined pathway that led into the park, and I could see the park lake across the level meadow in the distance. The sky started to get dark. Suddenly, I thought I heard someone or something following me. Every time I walked, I heard *jingle-jingle*. When I stopped walking, so did the sound. I was feeling spooked now; something was behind me!

I looked back, and in the shadows of a fall evening in the park, I could see something small and black running down the park entrance toward me. It was my cat Sparky—my seemingly only friend. That cat never followed me before. So I was so happy to see my cat. I forgot why I ran away. And now I was hungry, and I knew my mom had some hot food.

I picked my cat up and told him, "Sparky, don't you know this is no place for a cat like you to be wandering around all alone. Let's go home!" The two homeless men followed me to the edge of the dark park.

When I got home, no one was home. I was not sure where they were. It was quiet. I was happy my cat was home and safe. I was still hungry, so I opened the refrigerator to see if there was any food. What I saw was a half-empty bottle of Port Sherry.

I stared at the half bottle of Port Sherry for a minute and thought, *Nobody is home*, so I got a glass and poured some in. I took a sip. It burned the inside of my mouth and tasted hor-rible. I spit it out and reached inside the dimly lit refrigerator and grabbed a container of milk. *Ugggh! This milk is sour! Also horrible!*

Later, I found out that I had been drinking buttermilk. But the one sip of the alcohol had worked. I felt worry-free and relaxed from only one sip of it! I thought to myself, *My dad was on to something here. So that's why he drinks it!* My head was hurting and spinning, and I passed out.

The next week, my family and I went up to visit my grandfather at his parsonage house in Califon, New Jersey. There were wheat fields in front of his nice country-style home. The room I slept in had a tin roof. I loved the sound when it rained hard on cool rainy nights. I would fall asleep to the sound of the rain beating like a thousand drums on the tin roof.

In the morning, a rooster would crow at the break of dawn. In my grandfather's backyard, he had a white pet goat.

On Sunday, we all went to hear Grandfather *preach* at his Methodist church on this property also. Grandfather was a *fierce* and *fiery* preacher with over fifty years of experience by now on the pulpit. He was so fiery about "hell and damnation," it *scared everyone* in the congregation, including me! Grandfather recorded all his sermons on a "wire" recorder.

After church, we went for a big Sunday dinner. My grandmother had baked an apple pie. Grandfather said grace, and we all had a wonderful meal. Then we went back to my parents' house.

A year later, my grandparents came back to live with us again, and now, Grandfather practiced in the next town of North Plainfield.

One day, when I was all alone in the house, I got up the courage to go up to the third floor attic. I got a flashlight and opened the door to a pitch-black attic room. I went in. I bravely shined the flashlight around in the darkness. I saw some interesting things in a *cedar chest*. I opened it up. *Wow, what a nice smell!* Old sweet smell of cedar wood inside, a box of 78 records, and finally I opened one last big box. I shined my light inside. It was full of "heads!"

I screamed and ran downstairs.

That night, at the dinner table, I confessed that I went up to the attic and asked what the heads were. My mother said that they were puppet heads for church puppet shows. (It nearly scared me to death!)

When sober, my father was a nice guy and had a sense of humor. His favorite limerick was

> There once was a man named Sidney,
> Who drank till it ruined his kidney.
> He drank and he drank, and
> it shriveled and shrank,
> but he had fun doing it, didn't he?

My dad took me up into the attic and showed me the puppet heads again and also a complete set of marionettes from my grandfather's church. *He also showed off to me his pristine collection of 78-rpm records from the 1920s and 1930s.* He played one for me on a windup Victrola record player, "Five Foot Two, Eyes of Blue, Has Anybody Seen My Gal?" and another one, "Daddy, Won't You Please Come Home?" and lots of Annette Handshaw records, "Under the Moon."

When my father was a boy, Grandfather insisted that he learn to play music. My father had learned to play the violin and piano well. One cold night at seven years old, I was sick with fever dreams, and I was sleeping in my dark bedroom. And I could hear my father playing the violin and my aunt Judy playing the piano. "Dancing Doll" was the song. It was a *beautiful* song to sleep by—a very peaceful song. But father never taught *me*! I wanted to learn music too.

My bedroom was decorated with model airplanes, and it was located on the second floor. When I left the house to go to my big backyard to play, instead of going out the front of the house or the back door, I'd climb out my second-story bedroom window, slide down the drainpipe, and I'd be on the ground. I came back that way too!

I wanted to build a tree house in the corner tree. I put some boards up in the tree. Some neighborhood kids helped me build a platform to sit up in the tree, for boys only. I nailed sticks to the tree in order to climb up to the platform. One day, I was on the top step. The stick broke, and I fell to the ground. I've been afraid of heights ever since then. But I loved the view way up there.

Television was new in the fifties. I watched kid shows, such as *Popeye the Sailor Man*! I loved to watch Olive Oyl sing "Barnacle Bill the Sailor." Grandfather only watched the news all the time and seemed to worry about where the world was headed.

My grandmother, ninety years old, had the other side of the cellar that she used as a cannery. A special kitchen was down there so she could put peaches in glass Mason jars and make delicious homemade jams and jelly. The radio played "Heartbreak Hotel" by Elvis Presley.

One Christmas, my grandparents gave me a Lionel train set. My grandfather helped me build a huge model train display out of two old doors. It was very elegant, with trees, mountains, tunnels, and bridges.

My grandmother would tell me stories of her father Orlando Baker's adventures in Australia, Denmark, and Borneo. Grandmother could fluently speak languages like English, Spanish, Latin, and Greek.

My parents had a best friend, who became like an aunt to me! Her name was Aunt Peggy. My two aunts both liked to take me out with them early in the morning to go bird-watching. It was fun! They'd get me up at 5:00 a.m. We would eat breakfast and join other people, who were a group of bird-watchers. They bought me a wooden bird whistle.

One day, my grandparents brought over a female exchange student from Japan to spend the weekend at my house. This Japanese girl was nineteen years old and very pretty. I was only a kid. She called me into her bedroom so I could show her my whistle. She was beautiful.

When it was time for her to leave, the pretty girl from Japan kissed me on the cheek, and she gave me a strange gift: a handmade Japanese doll. She said, "You cute, Stuart! Someday, *I marry you* when you come to Japan! *Bye, Stuart!*"

So it began in the 1950s. I developed an interest in women, alcohol, *and* music by my father playing violin, piano, and hearing windup *Victrola* music of the 1920s and 1930s by Mae West, Annette Hanshaw; the 1940s with Frank Sinatra; and in the 1950s with rock and roll and Elvis Presley. It was not until many, many, many years later that I became an accomplished guitar player.

The stories of my ancestors and meeting the girl from Japan just made me more adventurous and curious about the mysteries and wonders of the world.

1952

Sparky the cat

CHAPTER THREE

The Parade

It was July 4, summer of 1954. Now I was nine years old. I had just discovered a thrown-away issue of *Playboy* with Marilyn Monroe in it. I liked what I saw!

Instead of wandering around unattended by foot, I was now a bike owner and rider. At nine years old, I would ride around alone up to twenty miles or more almost on a daily basis. The town was Plainfield, New Jersey. The nearest stores to my home had a boat store with a very large clock in the window. When you looked to see what time it was, you also saw his boats. The owner got used to me stopping every week or so to check out his boats.

There was a barbershop where my parents had always brought me to get my hair cut, with a large blue-white-and-red diagonally shaped pole in front of it. Inside, after sitting in the barber's chair, as a future self-centered alcoholic, I really liked what I saw! This barbershop had installed huge wall-to-wall mirrors on both sides of the room, and I could see an *endless number* of images of myself fading into infinity. I liked that. And on the corner was a classic fifties-style soda fountain shop where I could get chocolate or vanilla coke for a nickel and an ice cream sundae for a quarter. The place was called Ernie's Sugar Bowl.

I heard that the owner died of sugar diabetes. Next to his store was a general store that sold penny candy. I got a weekly allowance and also earned money from my paper route, which I spent in those two places.

Each morning of the week, a large bundle of newspapers would be dropped off for me to deliver on my bicycle. The route was about an eight-block area in both directions. Collecting the money from the customers was the hardest part but interesting. Once, a pretty lady opened the door and gave me an eyeful. And there was also a lonely and kind elderly lady who invited me in and had cookies and candy for me. And when I wanted to leave, she wanted me to stay. So things like that caused me to be late on my paper route at times.

But this day, it was the Fourth of July, in the morning. I felt like going for a ride to the next town, which was called Dunellen from where I lived. It had the nearest movie theaters, and most of the town was still a mystery to me. So I rode toward the next town, and I discovered I was passing through an industrial area which happened to be a Mack Trucks factory where I guessed they mass-produced what we kids called "Detroit dinosaurs."

On the other side of the road across from the Mack Trucks factory was a junkyard with a sign on it: Beware of Great Dane. I could hear a dog barking in the distance, but I heard something else as well. I was scared of the Great Dane dog when I rode by there.

Now I heard a new sound also in the distance. It sounded like music! The more I rode, the louder it got. It was parade music! Now I could see a sea of people ahead of me—people lined up on both sides of the street. So I rode my bike in and joined the parade. I started following different parade floats until I got behind some firemen who were on a float drinking beer. For some reason, this parade started and stopped a lot. These firemen had their hats on and were singing. Suddenly, one of them said to me, "Here, kid! Have a beer!"

After all that bike riding, I was thirsty, so I gulped it down. And instantly I felt transformed into a dreamlike dimension. The fireman looked fuzzy as he refilled my beer mug. I was in dreamland.

So I vaguely remembered the parade ended at a large park of unknown whereabouts to me. I ate a sandwich someone gave me.

Next thing I knew, I woke up in my bed at home with a bag with over fifty sandwiches in it. To this day I have no idea what happened or how I got home. It was to be the first of many so-called "blackouts."

But it was dark now. It was still the Fourth of July. I had a splitting headache. For the first time, I could remember I was missing the fireworks display down at the park lake. From my bed, I could hear the muffled sounds of the fireworks exploding in the distance as I fell back to sleep.

Stuart's Grandfather had a church here in 1902

My grandfather came back from the hospital and was now terminally ill. He was seventy-nine years old. My grandmother was now ninety-two years old. I was nine years old now. The entire family was home this day, and my grandfather was home in the downstairs bed. Little did I know then that *today would be his dying day.*

Aunt Judy grabbed me by the hand and took me aside and told me, "Stuart, I want you to go in and talk to Grandpa all by yourself. Just *you* and *him*. And don't forget to tell Grandpa that *you love him!*"

"Okay, Aunt Judy, I'm ready."

First, I sneaked to the kitchen, drank a small *sip of port sherry*, then a glass of *water*. Now, I was ready to say goodbye to my *grandfather*.

My grandmother was with the rest of the family, sitting in a big gathering in our living room.

I opened the door to Grandfather's room. He was on a big bed. The room was beautiful. I closed the door. Only daylight lit the room. He said, "I'm in *pain!* Pour me some more wine!"

"Hi, Grandpa," I say, "this is your grandson, Stuart."

"I know who you are," Grandpa said.

"I love you, Grandpa!" I said.

"I love you too, Stuart," he answered. *"Stuart, I want to tell you something."*

"Yes?" I said.

"I noticed your father is always putting you down, saying you will never amount to anything and you don't know what you're doing."

"I know that, Grandpa," I replied.

"It's not true, Stuart. Even if it is or was that way, it's not forever. *I know you will be a great, wealthy, and respected man someday!* No matter how long it takes, Stuart, always remember *Moses* of the Bible was eighty years old before he led his people out of bondage. And I'm not sure why, Stuart, but *I have a vision: You will lead people out of bondage also someday!* Promise me, Stuart, that *you'll never give up* trying to be somebody!"

"I promise, Grandpa," I said.

He smiled and said, "Stuart, thank you...call everyone in. I'm ready now." Grandpa had a mischievous glint in his eyes.

"Grandpa wants everyone to visit him now," I said.

The family gathered around him. Within ten minutes, he passed on to meet his maker. He was at peace. No more pain from his cancer.

I was grateful that my grandfather talked to me. He had never told me that he loved me before.

And I wondered why Grandfather had a vision that *I* would lead people from bondage someday.

Well, if I do, I thought, I hope it's before I am eighty years old, not like Moses!

CHAPTER FOUR

Ride the Waves

Holy Loch Scotland

I was seventeen now, and so far, nothing worked out. At sixteen, my successful older brother, who was seventeen years older than me, let me stay at his *house* in Massachusetts for a year, but I could not do the Latin home-work at school and could not relate to anyone there. I wanted to be alone. My brother's house had a huge backyard with woods and a stream running through his property. It even had horse trails. I noticed the tall trees in his backyard. Off in the distance, new homes were being constructed. I could hear the hammers. Another property next door used to belong to Henry Ford.

I looked again at the tall trees and envisioned a large tree house. I had built a small platform in my backyard once when I was younger, but *fear of falling* kept me on the ground. I asked my brother if I could build it. He said yes.

So with help from neighbor kids and scrap lumber from the neighboring construction site, an elaborate grand-style tree house was built. The scary part was climbing up the wooden boards nailed to the tree to get up there. The first step was six feet off the ground to prevent small kids from getting up there. The entrance to this grand tree house was a trapdoor on the bottom. It had a hinge that let me "padlock" the trapdoor when I was not there. Once inside the tree house, it was a nice room with a bed, a built-in desk, a skylight, two windows, and a bar, of course.

So I'd watered down my brother's supply he had in his bar in his house, using his bottles of alcohol, including Drambuie.

My early drinking days caused me, in sum, to accomplish nothing, so I went back home. Back at home in New Jersey, now at seventeen, I was a high school dropout with no direction or purpose in my life. I needed something different. I needed a change. What would I do now?

This was in 1962, and John F. Kennedy was the president of the United States. I liked him. So I thought, *I know. I'll join the Armed Forces… maybe the Air Force, like my older brother did.*

I'm not sure what happened next, but I mustered up some courage after a drink to go in to speak to Armed Forces recruiting stations. There were four all next to one another: Army, Air Force, Marines, and the Navy. I spoke to them all, and they all sounded convincing, saying to me that their branch of the service was better than the other. The last recruiter I spoke to was the US Navy. In that office, I saw signs that excited me, like Join the Navy and See the World! Now, that sounded cool and exciting. The recruiter was a clever fellow and observed how excited I became at the slogan.

Then he told me, "I've got another slogan for you, but first, let me explain something to you. The ladies who enlist in the US Navy are called WAVES. Okay, here is your new slogan. 'Join the Navy and Ride the WAVES!'"

"Yes, that *is* better," I said. "Sign me up!"

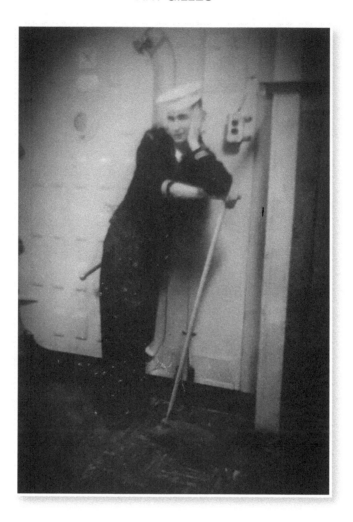

So I enlisted in the United States Navy in August of 1962 at age seventeen.

Next thing I knew, I was in Brooklyn, New York, in a large crowded room with a bunch of guys from all backgrounds, who had also just enlisted. It was afternoon now.

We heard some speeches, raised our right hand, and were sworn in to protect and defend our country, and we all were now officially accepted into the US Navy. I felt very proud for the first time in my life.

Next, nightfall was approaching. All of us new recruits boarded a train headed for Great Lakes, Illinois, for basic training. It was very, very cold there. I had a tough, abusive arm instructor, but I learned how to shoot handguns. I was issued a rifle, who I was told was "my new best friend," and learned to shoot and clean it and how to use a machine gun and throw grenades and how to survive fires and tear gas and lot of other things—and of course, how to swim.

Basic training ended in a graduation ceremony, where I was able to be in a parade again, sober, doing tricks with my rifle for my parents in the audience. It felt very good to successfully make it through boot camp alive.

Now, boot camp ended. Yes, I was in the Navy now! Now was the moment all of us were waiting for: our orders. Where would we be going next?

Fellow sailors and I eagerly opened up our orders. Everyone was going to different places, and some to schools.

I opened my orders: Report to the *USS Hunley AS31*! It was named in memory of a civil war submarine.

What was that? I never heard of that ship before. I had no idea that I was in for the adventure of my life. Turned out, the *USS Hunley* was a brand-new ship just built, and it was about to set out on its maiden voyage across the Atlantic Ocean. Destination: HolyLoch, Scotland!

The ship was a very large ship and was a "submarine tender." This ship carried *Polaris missiles* on board. Its slogan was *"We serve to preserve the peace."* It had lots of cargo cranes, but its main duty was to provide supplies and support to the US fleet of nuclear submarines that carried Polaris missiles. Two submarines could park on each side of this ship, and there was an unusual feature on this ship. On the back end of it was what looked like a circular railroad track, and what went around on that track was a huge structure way up high. And on a large cylinder way up was a bridge-like structure hanging in the air with a cabin under it. This feature on the *Hunley* was called "the boat and missile crane." The primary purpose and reason of this crane was to load Polaris missiles from the ship onto the submarines. The crane cabin on it reminded me of my tree house.

I arrived in Norfolk, Virginia, US Navy Base. I was welcomed aboard the ship, but since the ship was getting underway soon, they did not yet have a job assignment for me. So they told me, "Just take it easy."

The ship headed out across the Atlantic. The ocean was gray. Soon, no land anywhere was in sight. I'd never been on a ship before. This large ship was rocking side to side in the extremes. There was a warning to all to be extremely careful walking out on deck or else the ocean would get you. So when I did go out on deck, I held on tight to anything I could grab. It was also very cold, freezing temperatures. So my days now were spent looking at the ocean. I sat by a laundry vent to feel the warm air coming out. Soon, I worked at 3:00 a.m. in the mess hall making toast on a conveyor belt. The smell of the toast made me sleepy. And on one occasion, for about fifteen minutes, I was allowed to steer the ship, watching the compass, keeping it on course. How fun! A couple of times, the side-to-side swerves were so strong that all the tables and chairs in the mess hall and books in the library were thrown across the room. I held onto a post.

Finally, in January 9 1963, we arrived at our destination—HolyLoch, Scotland. It would appear our ship was relieving another ship that had been stationed there for three years already. HolyLoch was a beautiful, magical, peaceful place. I loved Scotland already.

CHAPTER FIVE

Scotland
Going Ashore

The *USS Hunley* was a gigantic ship about the size of the *Queen Mary*. From the deck of the ship, which was now permanently anchored in HolyLoch, Scotland, a large stairway and gangplank were lowered on the side of the ship. Small boats that had been carried on top of the ship were lowered into the water to be used as Liberty boats. Everyone was excited about setting foot on shore in Scotland for the first time. In every direction, the scenery was beautiful. The nearest towns were Dunoon and Gourock. You could see the waterfront dock across the loch.

Soon I was riding the small enclosed Liberty boat which held about thirty people, which bounced across the water, and in about fifteen minutes, it was tied up to a pier used by the US Navy. I was all dressed up in my dark navy-blue sailor suit with a white "Dixie cup" hat, and since it was cold, I wore my dark navy-blue peacoat. There was a small office-type building on the pier, and we had to show our liberty passes and Navy ID before being let out of the gate that led to town.

All sailors on the Liberty boat were out through the gate now. But we did not get very far. A group of people surrounded us, forming a circle. It was 1963. They were carrying signs and chanting, "Yankee, go home! Ban the bomb!"

A pretty female protestor kissed me on my cheek and put a flyer in my hand. It had a drawing with lines on it.

I folded the paper up and put it in my pocket. That drawing in the forthcoming years would become an internationally recognized symbol meaning "peace." The circle of people dispersed, and the protestors stayed peaceful and let us sailors be on our way. But as I walked by them, a pretty lady held up a peace symbol sign on a stick right in front of my face, which read Ban the Bomb! "You sailors kill people with Polaris missiles," she said.

Before leaving the ship, there was an assembly where we were given a lecture on how to behave properly when going ashore in Scotland. "Always remember, men, you represent America, so be on your best behavior at all times!"

I was hanging around with Gary, a fellow sailor who had gone to boot camp with me. As we entered a small cafe, I told him, "Remember, there are girls in here, so try not to use profanity. After all, we represent America."

Now before I joined the US Navy, I had never been intimate with a woman or used profanity, but over time, I began parroting other's speech. And now, I was starting to talk like a sailor because I *was* a sailor!

So we sat across from a couple of cute Scottish girls. In Scotland, we soon learned that the girls are called "lassies" and the guys are called "laddies."

We said "Hello, lassies" to them.

They were friendly, and they started talking to us with a heavy Scottish accent.

We knew they were speaking English, but we could not understand a word they said. As they spoke, their heavy Scottish accent was interwoven with Scottish words that were new to us. To top it off, these ladies spouted off a string of dirty words, including the F word, referring to another girl as a "bloody c——." That was enough to shock us and make us sailors blush. We got out of there fast!

I headed out to find a bar, which in Scotland they call a pub. I found one. I asked for a beer. The bartender kept calling me *Jimmy*. I said, "My name is not Jimmy."

He said, "All the blokes are called Jimmy over in Scotland."

I wondered what a bloke was! He then told me, "What you want is a pint of heavy!"

I said, "What's that?"

He handed me a beer mug that contained what looked like warm used motor oil. "This is what we drink here, laddie," he said. Then he added, "After you drink that, you'll need this!" He handed me a shot glass full of whiskey. The pint of heavy was a very strong bitter warm beer. It tasted terrible! The whiskey burned my tongue. But I could feel the ease and comfort as I was slipping into a euphoric state of "drunkenness."

"Where're all the girls at?" I asked.

The bartender said, "No girls in *this* town. For that, you need to go to Greenock or Glasgow."

Back on the ship, I got assigned as a deckhand because they had not yet figured out what to do with me. Mostly, I painted things on the ship, using haze-gray paint. One day, I was assigned to paint the bottom part of the humungous boat and missile crane. I kept staring up at the cabin, high up under the bridge-like structure, and at the crane hooks—a large one and a small one. I watched other crane operators drive it around. The cabin went in and out at the same time, going from one side of the ship to the other, using circular railroad tracks on the deck. I was fascinated! But I did not have a driver's license and could not even drive a car.

When the crane operator climbed down, I asked him, "Hey, can I climb up that ladder and have a peek at the crane cabin?"

He said, "Sure, go ahead!"

So I climbed up and looked inside. It was fantastic! I liked it better than my tree house! All kinds of windows and levers and buttons— it was nice in there! Most of all, up there was the best view of HolyLoch on the whole ship. I climbed down and went back to work painting. I realized up in that cabin was really the "crow's nest" of the ship.

I saw a Navy officer walk over to the crane operator. "Who is that guy?" he asked him.

In a couple of days, I got a new job I had requested—driving the officer's Liberty boat to shore at Dunoon. The officers' motorboat took getting used to driving. I remembered a childhood incident while driving an amusement park boat where I got it stuck in the boat track and even managed to turn the boat facing the wrong way in the kid's ride. And I had to dress nicely all the time because even the captain would go ashore in the boat sometimes.

Just as I learned to operate this small Liberty boat, I noticed that the officer in charge of the boat and missile crane crew wanted to talk to

me. "I saw you checking out the boat and missile crane. Do you want to come work with us?"

I said, "Yes!" That day, I joined *the Crane
Crew!*

I was happy with my new job, and it was
my turn to go on a three-day-long liberty pass.
So I decided I would go to Glasgow, which was
a large city farther away from the other local
town of Greenock. I wanted to meet some girls,
and that was all the sailors would talk about—
the Scottish lassies. I wanted to meet one too!

The Liberty boat going to Greenock was a
larger Liberty boat that looked a lot like a tug-
boat. It was painted haze gray, and inside held
about forty sailors. Scotland was cold this time
of year, in January of 1963. From HolyLoch to the
Greenock waterfront, the boat dock was an
hour's long boat ride through choppy waters.
When the Liberty boat landed in Greenock
at the Navy boat dock, I noticed outside the
Navy gate on the pier was a cafe called the
Jetty Cafe. It was open to the local residents,
as well as to sailors. The music played on the
radios, and jukeboxes in Scotland seemed to
have better rock and roll music than I had ever
heard before. Everyone in Scotland seemed
crazed and excited over a new rock and roll
band called The Beatles.

To get to Glasgow, I had to go to the
Greenock Train Station. I had a choice to take
a bus or a taxi. The buses were all red-colored

double-decker buses. This day, I took a taxi to the train station. Other sailors had the same idea.

I boarded the train, and it was not as I had expected at all. Inside the train was a narrow hallway with lots of little rooms in each train car. Each room on the train had windows you could see in there, and a door you can close. I checked for an empty room, but most had too many people in the room. Finally, I saw a room with one guy in it. So I sat down across from him. This man had a turban on his head and obviously was from some other country.

I said, "Hi."

And he said, "Hi," back. I had never ridden a train like this before!

The man wearing the turban was very friendly, and we got into talking about meeting women.

I told him, "Well, I've never been with a woman before. Maybe I will meet a nice Scottish lassie and marry her!" That is what I really wanted, which was not to be lonely anymore.

Then the man with the turban told me *his* story. "Well, I *am* married. But my parents picked out my wife for me when I was only three years old! I was not allowed to see her face until I married her. So growing up, she wore a veil and lots of clothes. So in my late teens, I told my parents that I was ready to marry her. The truth was, I could not stand it anymore. Curiosity was killing me! I just had to see her face and find out what was under her clothes. That's why I married her...out of curiosity!"

"Well," I asked, "did you like what you found?"

He said, "Yes, she is a nice woman."

The train pulled into the Glasgow Train Station. It was Friday evening now. I had to find a room in a hotel. I settled in and asked what to do in town. Soon I learned there were lots of nightclubs in town and also a very popular dance hall called the Palladium located in the center of Glasgow. I'd never been in a dance hall before.

I went into the dance hall in Glasgow. It was very nice inside—lots of lassies and couples. Great music and liquor were served. Some lassies were wearing *beehive hairdos*!

I wondered why there were so many girls there. Then I discovered that the admission price for men was high, but all ladies had *free admission*! So I got a pint of heavy and scotch and drank it.

I was feeling the alcoholic buzz coming upon me, and I saw a very pretty lady standing around, dressed to show off her firm perky boobs. So I was thinking, *I wonder if I should ask her to dance?* I kept staring at her and decided to order another drink, which might give me enough courage to ask her. I was sure I never stood a chance.

Finally, I timidly went up to her, tapped her on the shoulder, and in a squeaky voice, asked, "Would you like to dance?" I expected her to say no, but instead, a big smile came across her face. And she grabbed my hand and led me onto the dance floor.

"I'm Sally. Why did you choose me"? she asks excitedly.

I said, "What do you mean?"

She said, "There are lots of other girls in here you could have."

I was at a loss for words. I stared at her low-cut dress. "It's because you're so pretty!" I said.

She asked me to walk her home, and she told me she was leaving for the States next week. She kissed me. She was nineteen years old; I was still eighteen. We were standing in the dark outside her door, making out. She gave me a green garter from her leg. I was in heaven!

Back on the ship, I got back to work on the crane crew, wearing the green garter on my arm. I was proud of that! While waiting for my secret clearance to come through so I could use the boat and missile crane to load Polaris missiles onto the submarines, I was chosen for other smaller jobs, like loading supplies, motors, periscopes, and anything else that could best be handled by the boat and missile crane. For some reason, I was a natural at this job, and I loved being up in the crane cabin as often as I could. The officers knew I would always say yes if they needed someone to run the boat and missile crane.

So soon, another long weekend was coming up for me. Now it was February of 1963. So I decided to go back to Glasgow again, this time on the train. I was alone in a train cabin and thinking and wishing that I would meet the right girl in Scotland to marry.

I was taught that sexual intercourse was for having babies only. And both the man and woman should be *married*_first. And I did not want to get any ladies pregnant that I did not love and want to marry.

Now I was back in Glasgow. I asked a fellow crane crew sailor named Ricky, "Do you know of any place I can stay that I can bring a lady up to my room?"

Ricky said, "I've been in Scotland two years now. If you want to know something, *just ask me*! Yes, I do know a place. I have a room there too!" He showed me where it was.

I got a room across the hall from Ricky.

I said, "Thanks." I could see he already had a girl in his room.

I bought a bottle of scotch and put it in my room for later. Then I went back to the dance hall where I had met Sally, hoping to get lucky again. I went in there and got a few drinks, but there did not seem to be any ladies for me there that night. Soon the dance hall closed. Outside, it was drizzling wet in pitch black cold darkness!

I walked down Socki Hall Street (the main street) in Glasgow. I was thinking about going to nightclubs, when I noticed that two "unusual-looking" girls were standing across the other side of the street, staring at me and pointing. I was wearing a sailor suit. So I waved hello at them, and they waved back, silhouetted by hazy yellow light in soft rain.

The British young people were going through a fad of either being a "mod" or a "rocker." I was not sure what these two pretty young ladies were trying to be, but they both wore *sunglasses, black plastic raincoats, knee-high black boots,* and *black lipstick.*

I was half-drunk. I walked over to them and said, "Hi, girls. What are you up to?" It was about 3:00 a.m. now.

They said, "Nothing, how about you?"

I asked, "Would you like to go to a party with me?"

They said, "Maybe, we've never been with a Yankee before. Who is going to be there?" they asked.

"Well," said I, "the party is at my place, and it will be me and you two!"

They looked at each other, and then said, "Okay, let's go! I am Catrina. And this is my girl-friend, Amy."

The landlady where I was staying let me in and gave me a funny look as I brought Amy and Catrina into my room. I took out my scotch and gave Amy and Catrina a drink and, of course, one for me.

Amy and Catrina were both very beautiful. I was sitting in a chair and noticed they started kissing each other. I was wanting to join in, but they told me, "You can watch if you'd like to."

I said, "Sure!"

They got undressed, and I watched. And then Catrina said to me, "I'm sorry, Yankee, but we don't shag. We are saving ourselves for our husbands."

"I'm sorry. I apologize," I said. "I didn't know you were married."

"We are not!" she said. "Our *future* hus-bands! You sailors knock up girls, and then leave us. And we are stuck with the kid."

"Yes," I said, "you are right, Catrina. I do agree with you. I am looking for the right girl to marry. It might be one of you two."

Catrina said she and Amy know how to please each other in *safe ways* and can please me too. So they showed me other ways to sat-isfy ladies by watching them.

Amy was of Scottish ancestry with brown hair and blue eyes. Catrina's ancestry was half-Russian and half-Chinese.

Catrina said, "Don't worry, Yankee. Amy and I have figured out how to solve your problem too."

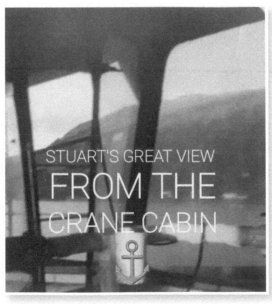

CHAPTER SIX

Stuart Meets Queen Anne's Ghost

Stuart's ship had three types of opportunities to go ashore to Scotland for "liberty" on the weekends. The first was work on Friday and go ashore on Saturday and Sunday. The second was to go ashore on Friday, then work on Saturday and Sunday. And the third was the best: go ashore all three days—Friday, Saturday, and Sunday. But to make that opportunity possible for the crew about once per month, I had to work. So now it was my turn to work the entire weekend of Friday, Saturday, and Sunday. My concern then was I had to go three days without an alcohol bender. Stuart craved alcohol badly.

As a respected boat and missile crane operator, I didn't have much to do. I was on call on weekends for any needs that could be solved with a crane. I was available to lift heavy electrical motors in and out of the submarine hatches far below my crane cabin. I also moved big objects, such as submarine periscopes and Polaris missiles, from the ship to one of the submarines. There were usually two nuclear submarines parked on each side of my ship.

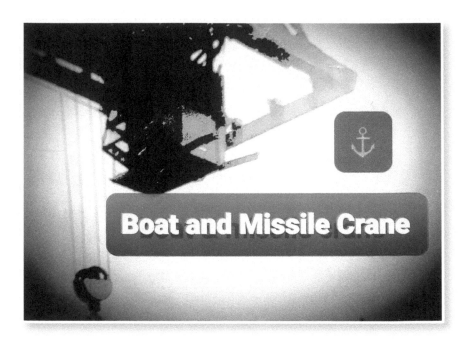

Boat and Missile Crane

So Friday night close to midnight, I got a call that one of the submarines was getting underway on Saturday morning. And around 2:00 a.m., they requested my help to load a new electric motor down the submarine hatch and to wait as long as they needed so they could change motors and hook the old one to my crane hook by a nylon rope strap, and then bring the old motor back onto the ship to the electric shop. I was an expert crane operator. I knew I was very good. I often practiced going full speed toward the boat deck with a nylon rope strap on the hook and stopping it an inch before it hit the ground. When I waited on other crane jobs, I practiced a lot, using both the giant crane hook and the small one, sometimes both at once. I'd have fun going around in a circle on the round train tracks while at the same time bring the cabin out to the end of the bridge, raising and lowering the hooks all at the same time. Yes, being in the boat missile crane cab was more fun than my tree house ever was.

I knew I was to work all night, so I went to the mess hall for coffee. And also, every night at 11:30 p.m., they served food, like a dinner, for those working at night. It was called "midnight tea." So I got in line with other guys for midnight tea, had a good meal, and was ready for work.

It was a freezing, below-zero night in HolyLoch, Scotland, but also a beautiful night with a dark sky splattered with stars.

I climbed up to a very high ladder on the side of the cylinder that supported the crane bridge structure and opened the door to the crane cab. I loved it up there. I had the best view of HolyLoch than anyone on the entire ship. It was a heavenly experience every time I was in that crane cab. This was a January night. My breath was freezing. I switched on all seven heaters in the cab. It got warm in there fast. While operating the crane, my view was through an open bottom window near my feet, where I could look down easily and see clearly everything below.

Before I went up there, I gave the electricians a strong nylon strap to place on my hook when the motor was ready. So now my crane was over the ship's deck. I dropped my hook and stopped it perfectly. So they shackled the motor to the strap and placed it on my hook. Soon, the motor was moving with precision, up in the air over the side of the ship, right to the destination over the top of the submarine hatch. Light was pouring out of the location of the submarine hatch, so it was easy to find. So the motor was over the hatch, hanging off my hook on a long nylon strap so that the strap would take the motor below the hatch where sailors aboard could grab it and work on it.

I was feeling good that night, wired up on coffee, and was pleased at the expertise of my crane operation. So the submarine electricians took the new motor off the hook and asked me to wait until they changed it out with the old motor.

So I was up in the crane cab relaxing. The strap on my hook was raised way up to the top to get it away from the submarine deck. From my viewpoint, I could see a Liberty boat coming into the ship. It was about 3:15 a.m. now.

Suddenly, I saw a sailor walking across the submarine deck below my cab. He was staggering and looked drunk. He had his white sailor hat on. He leaned over the lighted hatch. I was looking from above, high in my crane cab. Wow, I couldn't resist—a perfect target! I lowered the nylon strap down and knocked his white hat down into the hatch. Then I pulled the nylon strap back up quickly and silently. The startled and surprised sailor looked all around him, saying, "Who did that?" He was *very* confused.

After a few minutes, I then said, "Hi there, sailor!" from high in the darkened crane cab.

He laughingly shook his fist at me and climbed down into the hatch. It was a fond memory.

Next morning, I was sleeping in on Saturday. No calls for the crane meant no work. On this day, there was an announcement on the loudspeaker. "We have a special guest this weekend!" A British Navy's submarine would be docked here next to the ship for the rest of the weekend. So I went topside for a look. Sure enough, the submarine that was there last night was gone! It was already replaced with a strange-looking new sub.

Another announcement on the loud-speaker informed us that we are allowed to visit the British submarine and go on board to chat with the British sailors. Word quickly spread that unlike duty on American ships, alcohol drinking was allowed on this British submarine.

I walked excitedly across the gangplank that went from my ship to the British submarine. I was welcomed aboard. The British sailors were already primed with alcohol and were singing British patriotic songs. I was instantly handed a beer. I was enjoying myself with a beer. I was told that if I spoke with a British officer, I could get whiskey. After a few beers, I had the Dutch courage to speak to anyone!

So soon I had a whiskey in my hand, just for the asking. Soon I was in an alcoholic trance as it became Saturday night. Here I was in a British submarine, drunk, listening to loud music. Suddenly I became aware of trading going on. US sailors were trading their US Navy peacoats, sweaters, raincoats, and anything else for the Royal Navy's white sweaters!

I also fancied the hats the submarine sailors wore, which said HMS Submarine. The Brits wanted navy peacoats the most, and I didn't remember what else. So I went back to my living area.

I was drunk, and I was thinking I couldn't trade my peacoat. I might need it. I was thinking, *This is a once-in-a-lifetime opportunity. I'll borrow someone else's coat and get the guy another coat later.* So I grabbed a peacoat that was not mine and anything else I had that I thought I could trade, went back at night now across the gangplank down the hatch, and went back to drinking on the British submarine.

Next morning it was Sunday, and I had an alcoholic hangover. And I was wondering if it was all a dream, but among my possessions were a Royal Navy sailor's hat and a lovely Royal Navy white sweater!

I decided to go topside to see if the British submarine was still there. It was very cold outside. I went to grab my peacoat to put on, but it was gone. I learned that it was traded by another sailor who thought the same idea I had! When I went up on deck, the British submarine was gone.

Stuart
Macpherson

Crane Operator
Crow's Nest Cabin

I was up high in the crow's nest of my ship in the crane operation's cabin. As usual in HolyLoch, Scotland, there was a dark heavily wet pouring rain with lighted-up clouds behind a silhouette of shadow mountains, lightning and thunder abound. I was operating the crane that night at 3:00 a.m. to load some cargo from a barge parked alongside of my ship.

Another flash of lightning! What the heck! A blue-lighted outline of a woman's face appeared high up over the mountain. I heard a voice in my head.

"Stuart McPherson, I wish you no harm. Don't be afraid. I have decided to watch over you for a while."

"You can't be real," I said.

"I am as real as any ghost can be. Do you want to see me?"

Sorry, my new ghost friend, I have to concentrate. Come back later."

"No! It has to be now!"

BOOM! A giant white-yellow flash and a very scary face came out of nowhere. Her hair was on fire! Big grin! Eyes staring! I nearly jumped out the crane's cabin.

"You are not going to eat me alive, are you? You have giant teeth!"

"No, Stuart, I won't harm you. I am only a ghost looking for a new friend. I am lonely. I like to look after my friends."

"You look like a pirate," I said. "Who are you? Or should I say, who were you?"

"I am the ghost of Queen Anne. I was murdered by my husband, the king of England, who showed me no mercy even though I begged him to spare my life. But I am over it because a long time ago, I met another friend like you, Stuart. He is still my friend in the afterworld. He avenged me! He is Black Beard, the pirate. After I spoke to him in his dreams, he became a feared pirate, sinking British ships. Black Beard even named his pirate's ship *Queen Anne's Revenge* after me! How cool is that! Every time Black Beard sank a British ship, I would look down from the sky, very happy. Go get them! Thanks, Black Beard! I love him very much because he did for me what I could not do for myself. Goodbye, Stuart!"

Suddenly she was gone! The rain stopped. The dawn was breaking. The sun was rising over the HolyLoch.

CHAPTER SEVEN

The Lassie

Going to meet
a Scottish lassie ⚓

Back home on my ship, it was February 1963. I decide on my next Friday night, on my liberty pass, to check out the town nearer to the ship than Glasgow called Greenock.

I heard on the Scottish radio something that upset fans of the Beatles. They got a new drummer called Ringo.

63

The Liberty boat went on its hour-long ride, and this time, instead of taking the taxi to the train station, I took the double-decker red bus into town. I'd never been on a double-decker bus before. It was different. I entered it from the back of the bus. And another person, not the bus driver, gave me the bus ticket. I got on and climbed up the bus stairs to the *top deck*, of course, to check it out. This was fun!

Soon I arrived at the center of the Scottish town known as *Greenock*. I went to a small cafe in the center of the town and ordered a strange-tasting hamburger. The sailors called it a "mutton" burger. I ordered a cup of coffee, and I got coffee made with milk.

Soon and happily, I learned there was a dance hall in this town. So I planned to go there that night, and I did. There was *no liquor* served in this local dance hall. There were plenty of girls because as in the Glasgow dance hall, admission to this dance hall was free to lassies. Little did I know that it would be *here* on *this* night I would meet my first love.

I was very *shy* without any booze in me. So I stood on the side in the shadows of the dance hall floor. It was about half-full of people, and it was very cold inside. So I leaned next to a wall heater to try to keep warm. Then I looked across the room and saw *her*! To my eyes, what I envisioned was the prettiest girl I'd ever seen! As a teenager, I had a poster of a movie actress on my wall. The girl looked just like my teen idol! I could not take my eyes off her. It was love at first sight!

So motivated, I did not need "Dutch courage," so I walked sober across the dance floor and asked her to dance. She said, "Aye," which meant yes!

When I held her in my arms and heard her voice with the Scottish accent, I *immediately* fell in love with her. Her name was *Bonnie*, she said. I had just turned eighteen. And ironically this night, the *perfect song* was playing in that dance hall! It was the Beatles' "I Saw Her Standing There." I was a lonely sailor.

So I told her, "You might think I'm crazy, but I'm sincere about what I want to tell you. I know I just met you, but I *must* see you again. *I'm in love with you, Bonnie!*"

So Bonnie smiled and kissed me and would not dance with anyone else but me that night after I told her I loved her. Others, locals and shipmates, tried to cut in on us when we were dancing, but she told them all no.

I took a break to go to the restroom and looked at the signs to see which to use. The room I went in was full of ladies.

"What are you doing in here?" one asked. "This is *the lassies' room*. You want next door, *the laddies' room*."

I was embarrassed, but we all had a good laugh. My pretty Bonnie was out there waiting for me! It felt so good being near such a pretty girl who not only *did not run away from me* but held me tight, put her arms inside my pea-coat, and kissed me over and over. So I now was hopelessly in love, but I had to catch the Liberty boat back to my ship. I asked Bonnie for her address and phone number. Bonnie said no!

My heart fell. "Why not?" I asked.

"Well," Bonnie said, "I have to ask my mum first to see if it's okay that I date a Yankee."

"I understand," I said. I was worried that I would never see her again. I was going out the door; it was late! I had to get back to the Liberty boat or it would leave without me.

Bonnie shouted at me, "Meet me next Saturday at 1:00 p.m. at the Town Center Cafe!"

Back on the ship, I was in the crane shop with the rest of my crew. Ricky was there, asking me who were those two girls I brought to my room in Glasgow. He told me that Catrina and Amy came back several times, looking for me. I told Ricky that I probably would not go back to Glasgow for a while. I did not tell him why. All the other crane crew guys were older than I was. They were all talking about Scottish girls they had met. Rocky bragged he had a different lassie every night. The other two guys, Samuels and Horace, bragged they always hooked up with three ladies whenever possible: Irish Maggie, Big Lilly, and Hungry Hazel. Other sailors talked about these three ladies too. They were becoming sort of a legend. There were two other guys on my crew, an American Indian guy named George and a guy named Mickey who I liked the most. Mickey had the strongest handshake grip of anyone I had ever known. And he liked to prove it to anyone who even dared to shake hands with him.

On one Sunday, we were on duty together. Rumors about alcohol used on torpedoes for some reason was safe to drink with orange juice. It tasted terrible, and it was poisonous and dangerous, but we drank it anyway. So Mickey got a hold of some, and it tasted terrible. But we drank it anyway. It was a *quiet* Sunday afternoon. I got totally drunk once more.

On Sundays, tour boats full of people, including ladies, would go around my large ship and its docked submarines just to take a look. Our ship was a big Scottish tourist attraction.

Mickey and I were feeling the effects of the alcohol, and he suggested, "Why don't we go up in the crane again, so we can get a better look at the tour boats and maybe see some ladies!"

Having lost good judgment by drinking, I said, "Sure, let's go up!"

I went in the crane cab without remembering *why* I went up there for with Mickey. I switched on the motors, and within seconds, the crane cab was extended out to the end of the bridge, rotating in a circle, facing toward the tourist boat. As the tour boat started to circle the back of the ship, so followed the crane cab also in a circle at the end of the bridge until it was on the other side. We were waving at the tour boat. People on the boat were *cheering* us and waving back.

But the tour boat soon sailed off out of view into the distance. I parked the crane where it belonged and climbed down to the ship's deck.

Mickey said, "Hey, what is your hurry? It's Sunday. Everyone is ashore. Let's have some more fun."

"What do you have in mind?" I asked.

"Hook rides," he said.

So I grabbed the hook and rode it up from the lower deck to the second deck. Then I went back up and did the same for Mickey. "This is fun," I said. "But enough is enough."

He said, "Okay." Mickey was still a little drunk. He had an oil can in his hand and squirted oil at me. So I got one too. And we ran around for a while, shooting oil at each other. It was fun that day, and no one ever mentioned it.

In Scotland, it would rain or snow almost every day at least once—sometimes in the morning, sometimes at night, but pretty much every day. The sailors called the rain "liquid sunshine." The week was over, and now I could hardly wait to go meet Bonnie on Saturday. I told no one about her even though I thought about her obsessively every day and night. I wondered if she would show up.

Saturday morning, I left the ship and took the bus to Greenock. All morning I was waiting around by the cafe. I walked back to town, waiting for it to be 1:00 p.m. I kept an eye on the cafe but did not notice Bonnie. So I decided to go inside and wait for her. As I walked in, I saw her already in there, sitting at a table facing me. She had blond hair and green eyes and a pretty smile. She waved at me and said, "Hi." She had a scarf around her hair and a full-length brown coat. I sat next to her. Yes, I was in love, and I held both her hands.

I asked, "So what happens now?"

"I'm bringing you home so my mother can get to know you," she said. The cafe was empty except for one person in the back. "That's my mum." A lady in the back waved at me. We all had a cup of coffee made with milk. I paid for it.

"Let's go," Bonnie said. And all three of us got on a red double-decker bus.

Now we were riding out of town into the Scottish hills around the town. I was sitting next to Bonnie, and her mom sat about five seats behind us. I was quite obvious because I was wearing my US Navy sailor suit.

We got off after about a three-mile bus ride to a suburb of Greenock. There were connected Scottish tract homes going up the hilly road on both sides. We got off the bus and found Bonnie's house. As I looked down the hill, I could see the area of the waterfront where my Liberty boat docked. It was raining now. We went inside. Bonnie lived with her mom and dad and an older brother. The house was very cold inside, but in front of the living room sofa was a gas-fired fireplace. All the bedrooms were upstairs, three of them, including Bonnie's room.

The gas and electricity were powered by "shilling meters" in the kitchen. In other words, they put coins in to run their utilities. Bonnie told me I could stay the night there and sleep on the sofa. There was a television there which they called the "telly." Almost every station was the British Broadcasting Company (BBC), and lots of shows about the Beatles were on. I sat with my arm around Bonnie, and I told her mom that I needed to get back to the ship early in the morning. They told me I could walk down to the boat dock from where they live and that Bonnie would go with me. They fed me some Scottish food that night, and when no one was looking, Bonnie and I kissed and hugged while watching television.

In the morning, it was cloudy. Bonnie had an umbrella, just in case. We walked down through streets lined with beautiful Scottish hillsides, dotted with *purple heather* on them leading us down to the waterfront docks.

We were early, so we went into the Jetty Cafe on the boat pier. I ordered breakfast for both of us, tea and scones, and looked at the jukebox. Songs playing in Scotland were lots of Beatles; Cliff Richard's "Bachelor Boy"; and protest songs like "Blowing in the Wind" by Peter, Paul, and Mary.

I put money in it and played a song for Bonnie by the Beatles. I told her, "This is the *best* song I've ever heard in my life." It was called "Things We Said Today" by the Beatles.

I told her also that my ship would not stay in Scotland forever. Just like the other ship that left, the Hunley would be gone before three years' time. The good thing now was that I now knew how to get to Bonnie's house, and I had her phone number too.

It was very cold on the Liberty boat. I knew it was an hour-long ride, so I sat next to the motor to get warm. It was already a happy weekend, but in the Liberty boat this morning, they gave us hot coffee and donuts.

I ate the donuts and drank the coffee and fell asleep until the Liberty boat reached the ship. I climbed up aboard my ship just in time for "roll call." At roll call, it did not matter if you were drunk or sober, only that you *showed up each day and reported for duty.*

During the next week, two announcements were made: (1) that the Hunley was forming a boxing team and (2) that the USO people from the states were coming to entertain us on the ship.

I signed up to be on the ship's boxing team. I knew nothing about it. I wanted to impress Bonnie. Our ship's boxing team went ashore during weekday nights to train. It was soon announced that the ship's team would fight the Scottish national boxing team. One guy on the boxing team was a Golden Gloves boxing champion from New York City named Roy. Roy was of African American descent and was our instructor for the boxing team. Roy taught us all how to box and dance around the ring. Our other best fighter was a guy from Texas. He was a guy we did not care for much because word was out that he liked to beat up his Scottish girlfriend, and the craziest part was that his Scottish girlfriend *did not* want to leave him and always went back to him for more. They ended up getting married.

The big fight with the Scottish national team came up, and I decided I'd much *rather be* kissing Bonnie. So I told them, "Thanks, but I'm not cut out for boxing."

They said, "Okay. No problem."

The ship's team got clobbered by the Scottish national boxers, just as I had thought—all except Roy and the guy from Texas.

I was seeing Bonnie week after week now, rain or shine. I no longer took the bus but walked up the hills a few miles to her house. Sleeping on the sofa at her house was okay. But the fire in front of the sofa went out at night, and I was freezing. And now I walked alone to catch my Liberty boat ride because I knew the way there.

Bonnie and I did fun things week after week together. On this night, there was some kind of Scottish national holiday going on. She led me outside her house in the dark to the corner of the street. There was a gigantic scarecrow standing there. The people were singing songs, and all of a sudden, somebody lit the scarecrow on fire! People started cheering.

"What the heck is going on here, Bonnie?" I asked.

"It's Guy Fawkes Day," she said. I learned it was about some guy who tried to blow up the British parliament building a long time ago, and he was caught and burned alive. So each year, they celebrate catching him by burning him up again in effigy. They shot off some fireworks too.

Another time, Bonnie took me to Downtown Greenock to see a parade. Instead of what I was used to—a Saint Patrick's Day parade— here I was seeing the Orange Parade for Protestants, praising "King Billy." I grew to love Scotland and its people.

When I was home at Bonnie's house, I'd hug and kiss her and watch the telly until about 10:00 or 11:00 p.m. I asked her mother, "Would it be okay if I could come up to Bonnie's early in the morning just to say goodbye before I go back to the ship?"

Her mom said okay. So I came to her bedroom every morning to kiss her goodbye. Soon, because it was so cold, I got in bed with her. And we discovered our bodies kept us both nice and warm. So over time, our morning goodbyes became longer and longer until one night, her brother caught us in bed together. I knew everyone could hear me go up to her room because in the quiet cold night, the stairs squeaked. Bonnie smoked cigarettes. I didn't, but I carried a lighter so I could light hers. I also had lighter fluid. Back on the ship, I put oil into the lighter fluid can. At Bonnie's house, I oiled the stairs so that there would be no more squeaking. The relationship with Bonnie was platonic, except for hugging and kissing, because I wanted to marry Bonnie. The real reason I continued to cuddle up in bed with her was because it was cold, and I could not think of a nicer way to keep warm.

I respected her, and I wanted to prove to her that I'd marry her someday. I bought an engagement ring and told her I wanted to marry her but I did not know when. I asked her. She said yes!

I told her, "First, I have to let my parents know, and since I'm in the US Navy, I have to get their permission also. I proposed down on my knees and put the ring on Bonnie's finger. *We were engaged now.*

Back on the ship, I told everyone. Lots of sailors had the same idea and wanted to marry Scottish lassies because time would run out. Everyone would be assigned to new places. And the *USS Hunley* would go back to the United States for an overhaul, then it would go to Spain. I also wrote a letter to my parents back home and told them about Bonnie and that I wanted to marry her.

"Stuart! Report to the chaplain's office." Also, a ship's flyer *warned* sailors that many ladies were only marrying sailors to become US citizens and go to the States and that we might be being used by them. Then, I also got a panicked letter from my parents! "Stuart, you're too young to get married!" my dad said. "You don't know what you are doing! You need to finish college first."

So suddenly, red flags went up. Stuart began to wonder if Bonnie was the right girl for him to marry. He also noticed she was *not* into Beatles music like he was. Bonnie was at work now and has a job at a tin factory doing manual labor, putting things in boxes. I still loved her, but now I wondered if I should *wait awhile* before marrying her. I told that to Bonnie. "Maybe we should wait." She did not want to wait.

Stuart was supposed to operate the crane this weekend, but Ricky said, "Hey, I'm going to play cards and win some money. Also, Stuart if you need money at any time, I'll give it to you. Hey, if you want to go ashore Sunday, I'll cover for you."

"Yes, but I'm broke!" I said.

Ricky said, "It's like this Stuart. I give you five dollars. You pay me seven dollars back on pay-day. And I'll give you all the money you want at that rate."

Wow! Ricky was running a slush fund!

So Sunday, Ricky covered my crane duty for me, and he had money now. I headed over to Bonnie's house unexpectedly. Her brother told me she went somewhere with a girlfriend that she works with, so I went looking for Bonnie. Instinctively, I walked toward an unknown area of Scottish tract houses, and suddenly I see a phone booth with a girl standing outside it. Bonnie and *another* sailor were *together* in the red phone booth! She was with another guy! I was shocked!

Stuart went over and knocked on the phone booth. "What are you doing in there, Bonnie?"

The guy came out. He was a Filipino sailor who worked in the officer's mess hall. Suddenly, about thirty other Filipino sailors came pouring out of a house, and they formed a big circle around me and Bonnie while we argued. I gradually became aware I was being circled by all these guys.

Bonnie got mad at me and took the engagement ring off and threw it on the ground in front of me inside the circle of sailors!

Well, even if I could box well enough, I knew I was no match for thirty sailors, so I parted the circle and left for nearest pub for a pint of heavy. Bonnie broke my heart that day: a good reason to justify getting drunk! Stuart got drunk that night.

Back on the ship in the crane shop, I told my friend, Mickey, about my girlfriend breaking my heart. Mickey said to me, "Why don't you look up that girl in Glasgow that Ricky says is looking for you and wants to marry you too!"

I said to Mickey, "You know, that sounds like a real good idea right now."

Mickey said, "I'd like to go with you so you can show me where that dance hall is. I've never been to Glasgow before."

The long weekend liberty came again, and this time, I was not going anymore to see Bonnie. But I was going with Mickey to Glasgow. I showed and told him all about the train. We talked in the train cabin. Soon, we were outside of the Glasgow dance hall. "Here you go, Mickey. This *is the place*!"

Mickey said, "Thanks!"

Suddenly, my Navy African American shipmate Roy from my boxing team showed up. I told Mickey that Roy was a Golden Glove boxing champion from New York and now a ship champion because he won the fight against the Scottish team.

I introduced Roy to Mickey. But Mickey acted rude and pushed Roy to the ground. Mickey started calling Roy all kinds of names!

Oh no! What the heck is Mickey doing? He was trying to pick a fight with Roy on purpose. *Doesn't Mickey know that Roy is a champion boxer?* Mickey called him *insulting names!*

The fight was on, and I followed both of them to a back dark alley. Roy took a swing at Mickey, but Mickey grabbed Roy's fist with his vice-like grip. And soon, the champion boxer was helpless on the ground. Mickey let Roy get up, and then Mickey said to Roy, "Roy, my name is Mickey, and I apologize for calling you names and picking a fight. I just wanted to see if I could beat you. Let me buy you a drink." And both of them walked off together into the darkness of early evening. Mickey and Roy *became* good friends.

So now I looked at the paper with Catrina's address and showed it to a taxi driver in Glasgow. The taxi driver dropped me off in front of Catrina and Amy's house. I knocked on the door. It was Friday night. Amy opened the door.

"Hi!" I said.

Amy looked confused and *surprised* to see me! "Where have you been?" Amy said.

"Catrina's been looking for you for weeks on end! She loves you and wants to marry you!"

Amy invited me to stay there and wait for Catrina. I had brought a bottle of scotch. Amy and I started getting drunk. Soon Amy was crying and told me, "Listen! I care about Catrina, and I want to *make sure you will treat her right!*"

"I'll do my best," I said.

Amy said, "Did you like it when you saw me and Catrina making love and kissing?"

"Yes, very much so," I said.

"Well, *I bet you don't know anything at all about pleasing a woman,* do you, Yankee?"

"Now that you mentioned it, you are right! I don't know *anything!*"

"I can't have you seeing Catrina until you know how to please her."

"She is not here. But I could teach you what to do, and you can practice on me!"

I said, "Sounds like a *great* idea to me! I'm okay with it."

Amy led me to her bed.

"Stop! Wait!" Hold it!" I said. "I need *another drink first!*" I passed out drunk.

It was Saturday morning. "I don't think Catrina's coming home this weekend," I said.

"Do you want to leave?" Amy asked.

"Well, Amy," I replied, "to be honest with you, I think you're the best teacher for this sort of thing, and I'd rather stay with you."

I enjoyed my company with Amy. We had a good time talking about Catrina and about Scotland. I talked to her about the Beatles, and she said that the band members reminded her of Scotland's special cow, the *Highland Cow*, which had long hair and bangs. She showed me a photo of one, and she was right. It was similar. I spent all day and all night with Amy, and she kept giving me lessons until she was positive I got it right.

Sunday morning came before I knew it. I decided I had a good time and decided to check in at the train station early and get back to my ship by afternoon. I entered the Glasgow train station, got my ticket, and waited for my train.

In the middle of the aisle were a row of luggage lockers with keys in some of them. So I bought a newspaper and stood up, leaning against the luggage lockers. Suddenly, four guys came running into the entrance and *hid* behind the storage locker. A voice said, "Ahoy, sailor, can you help us out?"

"Sure, if I can," I said.

"Someone is following us. Tell them we went *that* way!" He points to the right side of the train station.

I said, "Okay, I can do that. Who is following you?" I asked.

Suddenly, I heard what sounded like a *herd of buffalo* coming toward me! They were *screaming girls*! I pointed to the right. They all ran that way. "Thanks," a voice said.

I went to get on my train. Now I asked the conductor, "What's that all about?"

"Nothing," he said, *"it's just the Beatles!"*

On my train ride back to Greenock, I knew I could not marry Catrina after my experience with Amy. I also could see that *Amy* was in love with Catrina, and I would not want to be the one to separate them. But I would never forget and would always remember those two and my train station experience.

So back on the ship now and over the loudspeaker was "Stuart report to go to see the ship's captain."

It turned out that Bonnie's girlfriend at the tin factory had a relative that was friends with the captain. The ship's captain said to me, "I've heard about you having trouble with a lassie on shore. I understand you were living there, and your belongings are still at her house. I suggest you go pick them up."

I told the captain what happened. "After that, I don't feel safe going up there anymore."

So the captain said to me, "Sailor, I'll tell you what I can do. I'll send you up there in a shore patrol van with two shore patrol police to escort you so you can go get your belongings from Bonnie's house."

The shore patrol van arrived at Bonnie's house. Stuart had two shore patrol sailor guys wearing an armband that said "SP" on it, escorting him to Bonnie's door.

Bonnie's mom allowed Stuart in. He collected his belongings, except what he wanted Bonnie to keep, and left driving away in the shore patrol van into the rainy day.

Back in the crane shop, Ricky told Stuart that a sailor told him he saw Bonnie dancing with another guy over the weekend. I asked, "Who?"

"I don't know him, but his name is Henry."

I said to Ricky, "He can have her!"

I had a nice 8 × 10 photo of Bonnie and her dog and decided to find Henry and give it to him. I liked dogs, but Bonnie's dog always growled at me and once tried to bite me. I was more of a cat person. I soon found Henry sleeping on his bunk. "Here you go, Henry, you can have her!" I said, and I gave him my favorite photo of Bonnie and her Scottish terrier dog.

On the *USS Hunley*, when it was anchored, the ship became more like a building. And telephone lines were connected, and Scottish-style pay phones were located by the ship's store in the lobby. Calls could be made to and from these phones. So a fellow shipmate found me at my living area and asked, "Are you Stuart MacPherson?"

I said, "Yes, that's me, what's up?"

"There is a Scottish lassie calling you on the pay phone, and she is crying. You'd better come quick!"

I went down to the ship's lobby and wouldn't you know it. It was Bonnie, crying and telling me she loved me and wanted me back and she was sorry and said it wouldn't happen again. Bonnie wanted me to move back in. So we kissed and made up, and I move my things back to Bonnie's house.

It was November of 1963 now. Bonnie and I were sitting on her sofa, watching the television, and the BBC broadcast announced breaking news: "President John F. Kennedy has been shot!" We watched the news together, and when I heard that JFK died, I went into an emotional state of shock. Bonnie told me I looked as white as a ghost.

Most all of Scotland loved President Kennedy too. Bonnie and I both cried together. I went back to my ship. The *USS Hunley AS31* had been sitting there in HolyLoch and had not been sailing out to sea for two years since its maiden voyage. It would be heading back to the USA soon for an overhaul. The captain wanted to make sure everything on the ship was in working order. "We are getting underway tomorrow morning. We are going to *Ireland* for seven days."

So the crew got all excited. I used the boat crane to load up all the small Liberty boats and put them back on top of our ship. We would need them to go ashore when we would get to Ireland. There were four small Liberty boats. I loaded three of them—only one more to go!

As I looked down as the Liberty boat driver got in position and put the straps on my hook, who did I see down there? It was Henry! I picked the boat up *high* so I could talk to him. "Hey, Henry, what were you doing messing with my girlfriend Bonnie? I got you now, don't I?"

Henry and his boat were hanging off my hook high up in the air. He had a concerned look on his face.

"Nothing at all!" said Henry. "Bonnie asked me to dance because *she wanted me to find you* and to tell you she loves you! She means nothing to me!"

"Okay," I said. "Thanks, Henry...I want my photo back!"

"Okay," he said.

I finished loading his Liberty boat on board. Later when I tried to get the photo back, Henry said, "Sorry, I can't find it. I guess I lost it."

Even so, I still could not view Bonnie like I did before. I always wondered if Henry was truthful. The ship was now leaving Scotland for one week.

The *USS Hunley* left. I could see HolyLoch fading from view as we sailed away. It was late November of 1963. The destination where we would anchor was off the coast of Bangor, Ireland, with the town of Belfast near to it. It was good to be out at sea again. I was amazed when the ship entered into the Irish Sea. The whole Irish Sea was light *green*! I couldn't believe it!

As the *USS Hunley* dropped anchor, I was on the deck looking at the Irish coastline. Everything was green! This was the *Emerald Isle*, all right!

Then I looked down at the Irish Sea and saw guys in rowboats coming out to welcome us. Some sailors were throwing coins at them. But the sailor next to me embarrassed me by shouting down to the guy in a rowboat. "Hey, down there! Do you have a sister?"

"Yes," a voice shouted back.

"Tell her I have a lot of money and a good one too."

Lucky for me, since I *loaded* the Liberty boats, I did not have to unload them. I was ready to go ashore to check out Ireland. Like Dunoon in Scotland, Bangor did not have much to do in that town. A friendly Irish vendor of a tourist shop that sold souvenirs such as a shillelagh, which could be used both as a walking stick and a weapon, said, "What's your name?"

"Stuart," I said.

"I'll show you how to fight with this Yankee," said the store owner.

I took a cab into town. I went into the bar. I got a big welcome from all the locals. It turned out that President John Kennedy was of Irish descent, so the locals all *insisted* on buying me drinks. It was Friday early evening, and I was already "smashed" in the Irish pubs. I played darts with the locals, and we talked about how great President Kennedy was. All night, Stuart drank double diamond beer.

Stuart wanted to check out the Irish girls, so I went to the Belfast dance hall. To my surprise, there were no Irish guys in there at all that night—only sailors and lots of girls. I was drunk and grabbed the dance hall microphone and made a speech about President Kennedy passing away. All the sailors and Irish girls paused and said a prayer for Kennedy and his family. Then I stumbled out the door.

When I got out the Irish dance hall, I remembered I forgot all about finding a hotel for the night. As I stumbled along the streets of Belfast at night, Irish girls would come up to talk to me. I was kissing one, and when I opened my eyes, it was another. I was pretty drunk. A girl let me walk her home, but she said she had nowhere for me to sleep. So it was 3:00 a.m. It was raining cold. Hotels were all full. I asked an Irish policeman what I should do.

"Well, you are welcome to sleep in our jailhouse if you want to!"

So Saturday morning in Belfast, Ireland, I woke up in an Irish jail cell, but it was not locked. I thanked the police department for their courtesy and left to go walk around the town.

It was Saturday now. I had an Irish breakfast. I felt okay. Suddenly, a bunch of ladies were coming toward me. I was wearing my navy-blue sailor suit with the white Dixie cup hat. The girls all surrounded me. "Can we hear you talk?" they asked. "Yankees talk funny."

"No," I said, "it's *you* girls that talk funny!" And I meant it. I could hardly understand them. It was like talking Scottish with a Southern drawl accent. I just loved to hear them talk!

It was a crowd of thirty pretty young ladies. In the center, one of them caught my attention when she put both her arms behind her neck to stretch. She had *bright-red hair*, and with her arms up like that, I could see she had red hair under her armpits. *How strange*, I thought. But she was pretty—almost like a redhead version of Bonnie.

So I went up to her and said to her, "Hi! Listen, my ship and I am leaving tonight, but you caught my eye. I was wondering if you could hang out with me today."

"My name is Katie," she said. "But I have to go home now. I'll meet you back here at 3:00 p.m."

Katie came back. We ate something. I drank another Irish beer. I paid, and we decided to go to the movies. In the darkened movie theater, I put my hand around Katie's shoulder. She grabbed my hand.

Oh, darn! I thought. But then she took my other hand and put it on her blouse. It felt nice. I did not even notice the movie. My hands also wandered to her armpits, and I enjoyed stroking the hair under her armpits. Katie loved it and kissed me. Now, drunken Stuart focused on Katie for now.

It was getting late now. I had to go back to the ship by 10:00 p.m. on Saturday. I asked Katie, "Will I ever see you again?"

Katie said, "I wish I could tell you yes, but I already have a boyfriend. And my parents don't like Yankees."

"Okay, then cheerio," I said.

On the way back to the Irish boat dock, I stopped and bought Irish souvenirs and my shillelagh. As the ship sailed away, the moonlit Irish Sea turned from green to dark gray again.

The *USS Hunley* arrived back from Ireland and, once again, anchored in HolyLoch. The end of our stay in Scotland was coming soon. Almost everyone aboard the ship was issued new orders.

I had new orders, and at the same time, I was promoted in rank from seaman first class to petty officer third class. I was assigned to a small warship that had torpedoes on it. Even if I could stay on with the *USS Hunley* after it would get overhauled in the States, I heard that the boat and the *Polaris* missile crane will be removed.

CHAPTER EIGHT

Under the Sea

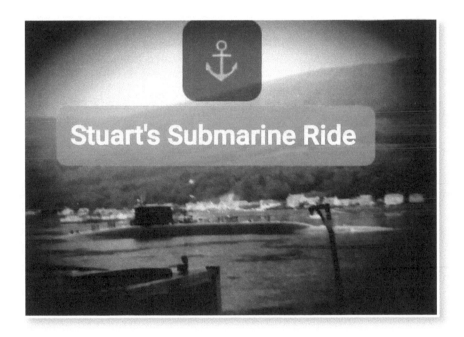

Stuart's Submarine Ride

I knew I would be leaving HolyLoch, Scotland, soon. I didn't really want to go, but transferring to another ship that may be going to other countries sounded exciting too. Before I left, there was one thing I wanted to do. I wanted to go down under the sea in a submarine. I heard that I could be allowed as a guest aboard when they would go out for sea trials. I put in a written request, and it was granted.

The submarines had two crews: a blue crew and a gold crew. Each would take turns cruising under the ocean for six months at a time, after which they got to go on vacation for three months, and then to work on their own submarine, getting it ship shape and ready for going out on their next unknown undersea voyage. The submarine crew wondered who Stuart was and treated him with respect.

It was Monday morning, and I was excited and ready for my submarine adventure. I crossed the gangplank, showed my papers, and I was welcomed aboard the *USS Abe Lincoln* as the crew's guest for the next seven days. I didn't have to do any work. I was told I could just relax, enjoy, and observe the submarine and crew in action. I was assigned a bunk area, and I heard commands and noises as the submarine cast off lines and was headed out of HolyLoch to the open sea.

I didn't know where to go, so I climbed on my bunk because I felt safe there. After about an hour at sea, I could hear the order to submerge: "Dive! Dive!"

I then heard all kinds of noises, creaks, and groans from the sea pressure as the submarine went deeper and deeper. It sounded like a tin can being crushed.

I was in my bunk in the submarine, and now I was becoming aware of my surroundings. I was sleeping next to a large curved cylinder. Suddenly I became aware that this was the very same submarine I had loaded Polaris missiles on. Was I sleeping next to the Polaris missile? And all the creaking and groaning sounded like the submarine was being crushed in by the sea pressure. I started to wonder what I had gotten myself into. I asked a crew member, "Is this normal? All this noise?"

He said, "Yes, don't worry. You'll get used to it." He also explained that one man alone could not launch a Polaris missile. It took about at least six men to shoot one off, but once a Polaris missile was programmed and launched toward its intended target, there was no stopping it! Stuart thought about the "ban the bomb" protests. I loaded them!

The food was very good on the submarine, and I was treated very politely by the submarine sailors. I was happy. I was sober now because if I were drunk, I might call them "bubbleheads," which would not be a very good idea at this time, so I was also very polite back to them. I felt like I was on vacation, and I guessed I was. No work—it was fun so far. In the evening, they had an area that showed movies. The crew was excellent on the ship; but Stuart worried that a missile would go off, killing millions of people.

The submarine dived deeper. I went to my bunk to try to get a good night's sleep, and I was just about to fall asleep when there was a very loud explosion right over the top of my bunk! Water was pouring in all over on me! I was in a panic. Whistles and bells and alarms went off.

Soon the crew stopped the leak by turning a wheel over the top of my bunk. They explained to me that only *some_*of the cylinders have Polaris missiles in them when the submarine submerged. They intentionally filled the empty containers with salt water to balance the weight!

The *USS Abe Lincoln* returned to park alongside of the *USS Hunley* in HolyLoch after eight days at sea. I enjoyed the trip. The captain and the crew of this submarine were not really sure who I was or why I was on board, so they were not taking any chances. They were very polite to me at all times. When I left the submarine, the captain shook my hand and gave me a *bronze* ship emblem as a gift to remember my adventure under the sea. Stuart remembered.

More important to me from my under-the-sea submarine adventure was that I observed simulated Polaris missile launch drills that during all of this time on the crane crew, I had never thought about the possibility deeply before that *the Polaris missile I loaded* onto a nuclear submarine could be launched and I could be indirectly responsible for starting World War III! Wow. What had I been doing?

Stuart got drunk again. Well, when I would drink alcohol, the thought of responsibility went away. If I was drunk, I wouldn't care.

CHAPTER NINE

Farewell to Scotland

Bonnie knew I was leaving Scotland soon. She looked up my coat of arms for my clan—MacPherson. She told me about the *one-of-a-kind cat that Scotland had called the Scottish wildcat.* On my coat of arms was a picture of the *Scottish wildcat* and a slogan that warned Touch Not the Cat without a Glove. Bonnie gave me a gift—my coat of arms—as something to remember her by. I shopped at the onboard ship's store and bought gifts there to give to Bonnie and everyone in her family.

I also remembered two other people that I didn't want to leave Scotland without saying goodbye to. I bought a thank-you card and two blankets that said US Navy on them.

Only two weeks left in Scotland, so I wrapped the two blankets up in gift wrap and put them in one box. This gift was for Amy and Catrina. I wrote a thank-you note also for them. So the next Friday, I rode the train for the last time to Glasgow. I was going there for one reason: to say my goodbyes to Amy and Catrina. First, I bought a pint of whiskey and drank it down to keep warmer. It was cold and rainy. I went to their house and knocked on the door. It was raining, and I didn't hear any sounds in the house—only the sound of the rain. Nobody was home. Well, they did not know I was coming, but I had hoped to spend Friday night here with them. So I placed the box with their presents in it by the front door where it would not get wet with the rain. I put the thank-you card under the door. The card read

> Thank you, Catrina and Amy, for being kind to me and giving me happy memories. I am leaving Scotland next week and wanted to say goodbye. The reason I did not come back is I love both of you and could not make up my mind which one of you to marry. I'll never forget you.
>
> Love, Stuart

While walking away from Catrina's house, a bum asked me for money. He was raggedy and drunk. The panhandling bum was an American but not with the Navy. He was elderly. He said to me, "Listen, pal, I was like you once. You'd better stop drinking, or you'll end up like me someday!"

Stuart heard him but couldn't stop drinking.

Now it was still raining. I was in Glasgow with nowhere to stay. I was in a different area of the city than before. I asked another sailor where I could get a room for the night.

The sailor looked at me, and a big smile comes on his face. "As a matter of fact, I just came from there. Go there now!" He gave me the address.

I went there and knocked on the door. It opened, and a sexy-looking lady answered it. I told her someone said to me I might be able to stay here for the night. She said, "Sure, come on in. Make yourself at home, sailor. My name is Irish Maggie. This is Big Lilly, and she is called Hungry Hazel." Now two other sailors were already there before me and were hooked up with Irish Maggie and Big Lilly. I paired up and spent that last Friday night in Glasgow with Hungry Hazel.

Wow! I thought. *I finally had arrived! These three girls were the ones all the other sailors had been talking about all this time!*

Hungry Hazel turned out to be a very nice lady. She was the least attractive of the three girls. I talked to her all night. I liked her. She told me she married a Yankee and he went to the States and never came back. I just held her in my arms until daybreak, gave her a kiss good-bye, and went back to my ship in the morning.

The last week in Scotland was here now. I had to catch an airplane ride next Saturday morning at Preswick Air Force Base in Northern Scotland, so this would be my last night with Bonnie.

I was at Bonnie's house now. Everyone in her family knew I was leaving Scotland. I was sleeping on the sofa. The fire was going. Bonnie sat next to me for a short while only. Then she went up the stairs to her bedroom.

It was only 9:00 p.m. Everyone was already sleeping. I was on the sofa, thinking, *Why did Bonnie leave me here? I was hoping I could hug and kiss her for a while.* So all night, I was wondering, *Why won't she come down and join me on the sofa?*

It was 5:30 a.m. now on Saturday. I had to catch my plane. I went up to Bonnie's bedroom to say goodbye. She woke up and saw me and said, "Why didn't you come up to my bed? My mum said it was okay because it was your last night in Scotland!"

As I kissed her goodbye, she pulled me under her blanket. She was totally naked and was ready to give me all of herself to me the night before. *She had been waiting for me all night long!* We kissed goodbye, and I took a bus to Preswick Air Force Base. Stuart knew as a gentleman that marriage came first.

I arrived at 9:00 a.m. at Preswick Air Force Base and showed the guard at the gate my orders, and he let me inside the Air Force base. I was taking the 10:00 a.m. flight out on an Air Force plane. I was getting ready to board the airplane when an Air Force officer came to me and said, "Sailor, I know you want to get home. But we have an emergency, and someone else needs your seat. Would you mind putting off your trip until Sunday morning?"

"Anything to be of service to my country," I said.

I went out the base and asked where the town was. I was wearing my sailor suit in an Air Force town! I went to a cafe and sat around. Then I asked. There was a dance hall here. So I went, but it was not like the others. This one seemed quiet, and nobody was in there. Then a couple of girls across the room saw me and came over. "We don't see many sailors here, only Air Force guys."

"What is there to do around here?" I asked.

They look at each other and then at me. "Have you ever been to Monkeyaround Castle?" they asked.

I said, "No, I've never even heard of it."

The two ladies said, "We want to go there too. Can you give us a ride there? It's about ten miles away."

I said, "Sure." I got a taxi and told the driver, "Monkeyaround Castle, please."

The girls told me we were driving through "The Moors," and it became so foggy I couldn't see anything. Through the fog, the outline of a real castle came into view. "We are here!" they said. We knocked on a big castle door, and it opened. We went inside.

A roaring fire was going in the fireplace, and tables were all around. It was a cozy type of nightclub. I got a bottle of scotch for myself and bought the two ladies a drink.

Music was playing. Smoke was in the air from people's cigarettes. There was an upstairs railing all around us and rooms upstairs. The girls I came in with disappeared. Now I was talking with a much older woman.

"I am Sandy," she said.

So I sat at her table. Sandy liked to talk. Finally, it was about 2:30 a.m., and she said, "Come on, sailor, let's go up to my room!"

I was thinking, *I'm tired, it's about time! I'm nineteen.*

Sandy was a very attractive lady in her thirties, and she liked to be in control. She looked me over and said, "I've never shagged with a sailor before."

We were *both* half drunk. We went upstairs. I could see from the rails the fireplace below and our table. I went into her room. There was a nice big bed there. Sandy took off her clothes and led me to her bed. I got undressed too and got under the covers. I was tired.

But Sandy had other plans for me. I was totally drunk. She proceeded to ride me like a bronco! She made all kinds of noises. I was as drunk as a ragdoll.

Then, her long fingernails clawed my back real hard! It felt good but hurt! Then Sandy looked into my eyes, and I thought she was going to kiss me. But instead, she started biting and sucking on my neck! Stuart started to wake up.

I was drunk, but now I was thinking, *I'm in a castle! Maybe she is a vampire! Oh my god! I'm in bed with a vampire!*"

"No, I'm not a vampire...anymore!"

I jumped up out of bed.

"Relax!" Sandy said. "I'm just giving you a *hickey* so you will remember me when you go back to the States.

I said, "Okay, Sandy. If that's so, thank you for the hickey. I've never heard of one before."

My portable alarm clock went off early. It was morning! I had to get back to the Air Force base to catch an airplane!

I woke Sandy up. "Sandy, thank you for last night! I had a giant hickey on my neck. Bye, Sandy, thanks again! *I'll never forget you!*" I said.

Sandy got up and looked at *herself* in the mirror. A surprised look came over her face. "What this?" she asked.

I said, "I wanted *you* to always remember me too, Sandy. It's a hickey!"

"Thanks," she said sarcastically. Then Sandy yelled, "*My husband is an Air Force captain!*" as my taxi left.

Later that Sunday morning, I was on the Air Force plane leaving Scotland, heading to land in Connecticut, then a flight to Newark Airport, and then I was home in New Jersey. Only now my parents had another house in Westvale, New Jersey.

My parent's new home was in a good neighborhood too. They lived two houses down from

New Jersey state senator Harry Jones. I had a two-week vacation before I report to my new duty assignment. I had lots of gifts—souvenirs from Scotland—including wool coats. Nice gifts for my parents. I also saw in my parent's new home an old friend. My cat Sparky was waiting for me.

The *USS Hunley* left Scotland in 1964, and when they overhauled the ship, the boat and missile crane was removed completely and was replaced by a regular-looking tall crane. I never knew why. But I liked to think it was because no one else could operate it as good as I could!

I had left Scotland, but Scotland never left me!

Stuart was glad to be back to the United States for a while.

Stuart never got tired of looking at the beautiful view of Holy Loch Scotland

CHAPTER TEN

Sea of Blue

Stuart went to his new ship. Two weeks of "liberty" vacation were over with. I was best friends with my cat Sparky again.

My mom drove me to Newark Airport to catch my plane to Norfolk, Virginia. At the airport, another sailor walked by. My mother asked, "Do you know him? He's in the Navy too!"

I said, "No, Mom. There are thousands of sailors in the Navy."

I missed Scotland and also the lassies there, and I was sad that I did not find the right woman to marry. I knew she was out there in the world somewhere.

My next ship was the *USS Onion DD2214*, an older destroyer built in World War II.

I reported for duty. I was one rank higher now than on my other ship. I was a torpedoman third class petty officer. The only thing I knew about torpedoes was what I learned in the study guide book before I took the written test to advance in rank. I also took a general education development test for high school equivalency and passed it without studying or having completed high school for real. So I had my GED high school graduation equivalent.

Stuart hated being the new guy aboard. The ship was anchored in Norfolk, Virginia, getting ready to cruise the Caribbean Sea. The ship hauled up the anchor and set out to sea. First, to Florida. It was exciting because we were able to dock in Downtown Miami. The boat pier there was within walking distance to downtown. I saw the sights, got postcards to send home, and I also sent a postcard to Scotland. I had Bonnie's address; after all, I lived there for a couple of years. I had no girlfriend now. And I was not really sure if Bonnie was the right girl for me to marry. I wrote her every day. I had told my parents about Bonnie, and of course, they were against the idea of me marrying her. And I was not sure if I was really still in love with her. I had an idea that if my parents met her in person, they would help me decide.

Maybe they would like her. Stuart's parents said if she did come over, I would have to pay for the trip and all. If she did come over, she could *not* stay there at their house. Stuart had to find her another place.

So I called up my aunt Judy who said, "Sure." My aunt Judy was a Quaker and worked as a librarian. "She can stay with me," Aunt Judy said. But Bonnie never answered my letters.

In Miami, I was on liberty. It was hot, unlike Scotland. Instead of wearing navy blues, Stuart wore *white* sailor suits now. I went into a burlesque show that night. I was the only sailor in the audience. I was drunk, and the dancer came over to my seat. She was wearing a feather boa. She took it off herself, put it around my neck, and led me by the hand up on stage. I was drunkenly dancing with her in front of an unknown audience, but I was feeling *really, really dizzy*. The world was spinning around! So I had one more drink and decided to get back to my ship. I told her, "Thank you, but I have to go!"

Stuart Gets Alcohol Poisoning

Now the alcohol I drank was hitting me hard. I was staggering down Biscayne Boulevard in downtown Miami, walking in the direction of my ship. My eyes were blurry, and my head really hurt. I threw up in some bushes. My brain was throbbing. Finally, I got to the Fifth Street Pier, and I could see my ship's gangplank entrance about a quarter of a mile away in the lighted darkness.

Without warning, the pavement of the road jumped in the air and hit me hard right in my face! I was down! The world was spinning even faster. It felt like an ax was in the back of my head! I was feeling panic now because I realized and remembered *the warnings* about drinking too much *alcohol. I can't get up! I can't move! Please, God, don't let me die!*

I was afraid because I knew and I was aware of all the symptoms, and blood was on my face from falling down on the pavement. *I realized I might die tonight. Alcohol poisoning!* Suddenly, I passed out. Everything turned black.

Did I die? No, but I came very close. I was lucky. The ship's doctor said they carried me aboard and kept an eye on me until I came to. The ship's doctor confirmed what I had thought. He said, "Sailor, you came *that close* last night to *dying of alcohol poisoning. I suggest you stop drinking alcohol.*"

God, I promise I won't drink again!

My head hurt and was still throbbing. "Yes, Doctor," I said. "After last night, I never want to drink again, and I mean it!"

So during the course of the week, I felt better, although I was still a little groggy.

The ship was out to sea again, headed for the Caribbean Sea. At sea, I saw steam on the top of the waves and flying fish. The ship steamed past Cuba. It was not supposed to go in closer than one hundred miles, but the captain would speed in with the ship to dump garbage. The ship would chase rain clouds so the sailors could scrub down the ship. It was very hot in the Caribbean. The ship was conducting day-and-night crazy war games. I loaded big guns—loud noises in my ears.

The ship practiced war games in the Caribbean in preparation to go to Vietnam. The only thing I did not like about the duty on this ship was that there was one sailor in the torpedo shop, same rank as me, trying to boss me around because he has seniority he said. His name was Sam.

The ship was cruising fast across the sea. The *USS Onion* shot topside big guns with very *loud bangs*! I was below the gun turret, on the line handling the foot-long gunpowder shells, passing them to the next sailor as they fired at a deserted island. At night, flare guns would light the sky while the ship's guns continued to bombard the tiny island.

On another day, I learned how to prepare and launch torpedoes. We had unexpected simulation drills all the time to practice for duty in Vietnam. My enlistment in the US Navy officially would end the day before I turned twenty-one. I was now nineteen.

Stuart Goes to Jamaica

After ten days of solid war games, the captain announced to a happy crew, "We are going ashore for some R and R," which stood for rest and relaxation!

While back in Miami, cargo was taken aboard the ship and now sat in the back of the torpedo room. Nobody knew what it was in the boxes.

The loudspeaker said, "We are going to Jamaica!"

The ship entered Montego Bay in Jamaica. We were excited! Sailors, including me, were working up on deck to secure the ship with nylon ropes and tied it up to the Jamaica waterfront dock. The boxes were unloaded in Jamaica and given to local Jamaicans as a gift. They were cases of Listerine!

There were lots of street music onshore, playing of steel drums, and the sounds of gourds rattling to the beat. The steel drums were made out of old oil barrels. The music was quite good.

I was ashore now—lots of street vendors selling souvenirs, lots of kids asking for change, and a few beggars. As I walked into town, there were a couple of bars. But I had promised myself I'd stay sober.

I passed by all the bars and was on the other side of town when two signs on two different buildings caught my eye. One sign read USO. The other sign read YMCA. So I chose to go into the one that said YMCA. *This looks like a safe place for me to go into*, I was thinking.

I entered the YMCA and sat down. It was dark inside, and two ladies sat on each side of me. "Can you buy us drinks?" they asked me.

Without thinking, I said, "Sure!" And before I knew it, three alcoholic drinks were in front of us. Steel drum music was playing. Other ladies were on stage, topless and dancing. *I'm drunk again*, I was thinking. *What kind of YMCA is this?*

The first two ladies departed because I was not interested to go to bed with them. I saw a cute lady working back in the kitchen. I asked, "Can I speak with her?"

They said yes. They called her over. We went back into a private room behind the kitchen. I was feeling quite drunk, so I knew from the last time that I could not drink anymore. I did enjoy meeting her. She was good company to talk to, and we were only chatting. She told me the signs on the two buildings were to attract US sailors. It was not a *real* YMCA or USO. She said when the Russian ships would come, they would have signs for them in Russian to lure the Russian sailors in there too!

Stuart got drunk again. I staggered back to the ship, hoping I'd make it there. I did. We went out to sea again for another week or two of more war games into the Caribbean Sea.

I was up on deck with a hangover the next morning. The ship was going full speed ahead. We could see the long white wake behind it. I was in a hidden area, standing outside on deck by the torpedo room. Sam came over to me, shouting orders at me like a storm trooper! I said, "Not now, Sam. I've got a headache!"

He didn't listen but continued. Then he started shouting at me, *close up, right in my face*! I was annoyed. Sam was a short guy but made a lot of noise. I got angry and picked him up off the deck, holding him high in the air as if I was going to throw him overboard into the sea—crazy hangover from alcohol.

I remembered where I was and who he was, and I put him down. "Sorry, Sam," I said. "I didn't have my coffee yet!"

Sam *never* bothered me again!

The ship was due for a liberty break again. We had been out at sea for a week of war games now. Time for more R and R. The crew wondered where we would be going next.

The loudspeaker went off. "Our next liberty will be in San Juan, Puerto Rico."

We all cheered! "I was not drinking alcohol this time," said Stuart.

I was concerned that if I went ashore, I might get too drunk. An officer called me over and said to me, "Hey, Stuart! We need some shore patrol police to check up on our guys when they are on liberty ashore."

"What would I do?" I asked.

"Well, you will be wearing an armband that says "SP" for shore patrol on it. And you'll be carrying a gun and a nightstick. Your job will be to go to all the bars to see if our sailors are behaving themselves. If not, you need to arrest them and bring them back to the ship," said the officer.

"Okay," I said, "I'll do it." I was thinking, *This way, I'll be sure not to get drunk tonight!*

About ten of us arrived in our shore patrol outfits. We assigned ourselves different areas to work. There was a 10:00 p.m. curfew for the sailors. We made our rounds and chased sailors back to the ship. All the shore patrols were done.

The officer said to me and another sailor, "Listen, you two! There are still five more bars that are *off limits* to sailors. Before you go off duty, would you mind checking those out?"

We said, "Not at all, sir!"

At the first bar we checked, the bar owner met us at the door and told us, "Welcome!" and that because we *were shore patrol*, the *drinks were free* and we could *choose any girls we wanted and have them for free too*!

I said, "Thanks, but no, thanks."

But the other sailor said to me, "We can have *one drink*, and then leave. One drink won't hurt you, Stuart. It's *Saturday night* in Puerto Rico! Wake up and have some fun!"

Stuart said, "I guess only one drink won't hurt."

A shot glass of whiskey appeared in front of me. I gulped it down. Suddenly, two Puerto Rican girls were on each side of me, and there were two others with my friend. The *free* drinks kept coming, and I was hugging and kissing both girls. And my friend *was doing the same to his two girls*.

All of a sudden, someone shouts *loudly*, "Shore patrol!" It was four of the others. They came looking for us.

"We thought you were in trouble!" they said.

"I was," I said. "Thanks for getting me out of there!"

Next morning, we were back to the Caribbean Sea again for more war games. When the ship goes into a seaport, mail was brought aboard. Every once in a while, I would get a letter. I had one week's vacation coming to me when I needed it.

I had not gotten any letters from Bonnie at all—nothing! This was even though *I wrote her several times per week.* But then I heard an announcement: "Mail call! Stuart, you've got mail!"

The letter is from Aunt Judy! She wrote,

> I've been in contact with Bonnie's mum in Scotland and also with Bonnie. I have paid for Bonnie's ticket. She is coming to the States for thirty days! She will stay with me. Put in for your liberty pass right away!

I was *stunned* and *excited*! *Bonnie was coming! Maybe I should marry her as soon as I see her again!* I thought to myself. I was now thinking...I was feeling that I *loved her again* and *I am obsessed again.*

Wow! Bonnie is coming! I'm tired of being lonely. I need to find myself a good wife. I have Aunt Judy's phone number. I must move fast! I have to get permission to go home on a liberty pass.

Yes, I had the liberty pass now. When the ship would dock in Norfolk, Virginia, I could go home. But first, my ship had *one* more stop before going back to the States.

The ship anchored at the US Navy base in *Guantanamo Bay, Cuba*. Since the Cuban Missile Crisis, sailors could no longer go into Cuban towns. So when the ship landed in Gitmo, there was nothing to do but walk around or get drunk. For some reason, there was no telephone service either, and *now I knew Bonnie was at Aunt Judy's house*. Another sailor stationed at Gitmo said, *"I am a shortwave radio operator*. I can call another shortwave operator in New Jersey, and that way, you can make your phone call. *But there is a catch."*

"What's that?" I asked.

"You can only speak to one person at a time. When you are finished, you say, 'over,' and then it's the other person's turn to speak. And when they finish, they say, 'over.' That way the shortwave radio operator can switch a switch for you. *When you've finished, you say, 'over and out.'"*

"Let's do it!" I said.

That night, I called Aunt Judy and was also able to speak to Bonnie. "I'm coming to see you next weekend, Bonnie! *Over."*

"I love you! Over," said Bonnie.

"Over and out!"

My airplane landed at New York City Airport. I only had seven days. I was in a hurry to get to Aunt Judy's so I could see Bonnie! I took a bus from New York City to New Jersey to the town where my aunt lived.

It was Monday at around 9:00 a.m. I arrived and knocked on my aunt Judy's front door. *Bonnie opened the door.*

Bonnie told me that for three weeks, she had been sleeping on Aunt Judy's *sofa.* She explained she already met both of my parents and that Aunt Judy had given her quite a tour of all the sights of New Jersey. Aunt Judy even took Bonnie for a tour of the United Nations Building and the Statue of Liberty in New York.

I had some gifts for Bonnie and everyone else from my travels, and Bonnie had brought some gifts for me too from Scotland. After Bonnie opened her gifts, Bonnie said, "*I have a gift for you too! I have something very special I got just for this day.*"

"What is it?" I asked.

Bonnie reached in her travel bag and pulled out a bottle of *Glen Livet scotch whiskey.* "It's the best!" she said.

I sat on Aunt Judy's sofa, and Bonnie got shot glasses and poured both of us a drink. I slept like a rock until the next morning. Bonnie had slept in the room with Aunt Judy. In the morning, Aunt Judy fixed us some breakfast. She was a good cook. I had coffee too. I was sober now and felt good.

As Aunt Judy left for work, she said, "I'll be home early today, Stuart. We are going over to your parents' house tonight for dinner."

Bonnie and I walked together to the nearest store, and I bought us some snacks and another bottle of scotch. We had a drink and watched TV.

"*Bonnie, something has been bothering me,*" I told her.

"What's what?" she asked.

"*Bonnie, since I left Scotland, I've been writing you letters almost every day. How come you never wrote back to me, not even once?*"

Bonnie dropped her drink and looked shocked. "*What?*" she said. "*I never ever got even one letter from you! I thought you had jilted me!*"

Bonnie suddenly came to a realization. "*It's my mum!* She was reading all your letters and hiding them from me. Once, I thought I saw one in a stack of mail, but Mum told me it was not for me. When Aunt Judy wrote to my mum and invited me over to the States, *it's only then I learned that you might still want to marry me!*"

Bonnie told me that for the past three weeks, besides seeing all the tourist sites in New York City and New Jersey with Aunt Judy, they had also visited my parents several times so they could "check her out." They *did not approve* of her smoking cigarettes. I knew my father was a pipe smoker. So I ran down to the corner store, got myself a pipe so I'd smoke too in support of Bonnie.

My aunt drove us to my parents' house. Now it was time for dinner. *My mother was a very good cook.* The table was set formally with a tablecloth and with knives and forks in their proper place and flowers in the center— *all very nice.* I was wearing my white sailor suit. *Bonnie was sitting next to me.* I looked at my parents and said to them, *"Bonnie and I want to get married!"*

"That's all very fine," my father said. "But don't you think you should complete your college education first?" My father went to the fridge and drank some Port Sherry, and then finished his dinner.

My father stood up in front of all of us and said, *"You know, Stuart. You are the black sheep of our family! You can't do anything right! I told you, you would not amount to anything!"* My father continued to berate us. *"Bonnie is not on the same status level as our family tree. You can't even pick the right woman to marry! Stuart, if you still want to marry her, at least wait a couple more years!"*

Then my mother chimed in. "Stuart, if you really love Bonnie and she really loves you, it will only be a couple of years until you finish college." *Little did anyone know that it would take thirty-five years more before I actually completed my education!*

Aunt Judy drove us back to her house. *We had one more day together before I went back to my ship.*

We sat on the sofa. We got out the scotch whiskey we had hidden, and I said, "I *really need* a drink. Don't you, Bonnie?"

"Aye!" she said. "I want to marry before I'm twenty-four."

It was time to go. We said our goodbyes again. Next morning, both Bonnie and Aunt Judy came along to drive me to Newark Airport. We kissed a teary-eyed *goodbye.* They watched as my plane disappeared into the sky. I was sad, looking down on the ground from my airplane window at the dot that was the airport.

Back on my ship, soon to be discharged from the Navy about three months later, I got mail! It was a letter from Aunt Judy! The letter was telling me that *Bonnie got married to somebody else!* Aunt Judy said, "Bonnie, who was twenty years old, *is married to a Scottish man—a thirty-five-year-old man named Jimmy! He is her boss at the tin factory where she worked!*"

I thought I loved Bonnie, but now she was *somebody else's wife!*

I was devastated and brokenhearted. I drank as often as I could over that for many years. I was not sure why, but *it was a good excuse to get drunk* for me to feel sorry for myself. "God, *please send me the right woman for me to marry!"* Stuart prayed for the right woman to come.

I was a "short-timer." I was to be discharged out of the US Navy soon. I got orders to report to the US Navy base to the recruitment office. My duty time would be over in a month.

CHAPTER ELEVEN

The Village Sailor

The Navy officer recruiter said, "We have looked over your records, and we like you. And we want you to reenlist in the US Navy for another four years. It's a great career. You can sign up today for active duty or join the Navy reserves. That's your best deal. The other choice is for inactive Navy reserves, where you are still in the US Navy, but unless the Vietnam War gets a lot worse, you will not be called to duty. What do ya say, sailor?"

"I don't know," I said. "*I want to go to college.*"

"Tell you what. We can pay for your college education!" he answered. "Sign up for the *inactive Navy reserves* in the Navy for another four years today, and we will promote you in rank. And also, I see by your service record that you've earned *two* service ribbons that you have not gotten yet. We'll get them for you. Plus, we'll also give you $1,000 *as bonus pay!*"

"Okay, sign me up!" I agreed. I signed up for two more years in the inactive Navy reserves.

So the day came when I left the ship to go home. I now had the coolest US Navy blue uniform with bell-bottom pants. It had the two color-coded service ribbons pinned over my pocket and torpedo second class *stripes* on the side of my arm. When I opened the cuffs of my navy-blue uniform, *dragon* designs were embroidered on the inside of my sleeve. I toted my *seabag* over my shoulder and caught the airplane to New York City Airport. The year was 1966.

Stuart Meets the Hippies

I arrived in New York City. I thought to myself, *I've got the coolest-looking Navy uniform on. Plenty of money. I am still in the Navy but have no duty anymore. I'm free! What is my hurry?* I was asking myself. I went to the bus terminal, where later I planned to head back to New Jersey by bus, and placed my *seabag* inside a storage locker. But tonight, I planned to stay here in New York City.

I got into a taxi. I asked the driver, "Where can I go for fun in this town?"

He looked back at me, saw my uniform, and asked, "Have you ever been to *Greenwich Village*?"

"No," I said, "take me there!"

123

So the driver dropped me off in the middle of the village. I was not sure where to go or what to do. I grabbed a free newspaper entitled *The Village Voice*. I saw an ad for the crazy village coffee place. *Sounds good*, I was thinking. *I can use a good cup of coffee!*

The village coffee place was crowded with strange-looking people inside, which now included me in my sailor suit. *It was dark and dingy*. The coffee was black and strong. *The cups looked dirty* as if no one had ever washed them. On stage was *live music playing*, and it was *good music*. The songs were all *war protest music*. One guy got up and sang "International Sailor." The girl sitting across my table sang "Puppets of War."

It seemed like *anyone* who wanted to could get up, speak, sing, or read poetry! *How cool!* I thought. I loved the protest music. It was great! I was not completely sure what they were protesting about, but I liked it. From my table window, I could see outside the coffee shop. Standing across the street, two weirdly dressed individuals that looked like they were going to a masquerade party were there. One was taller than average, and I guessed he was wearing stilts. They were holding what looked like some kind of tickets in their hand. Every twenty minutes or so, maybe, they would give one to someone passing by.

When the girl across my table was done singing her protest song, I said, "That's great! I loved your song!"

"Thanks," she said. "I'm Joanie."

"I'm Stuart," I replied.

"What are *you* going to do up there on stage?" she asked me.

"Well, I just came to listen," I said.

"*Come on*," she said. "It's fun! I write music and poems. Go up and read one of mine or write one of your own. It's easy!" She smiled and winked at me.

I read Joanie's poems. They were *very good!* "I liked them," I said. "*But I'll write one of my own. Is that okay?*"

Joanie was excited. "I want to hear *your* poem, Stuart!"

There was a break in between the singers. Joanie said, "Go on, Stuart! *You're up!* Everyone in the coffee place is anti-war—no longer called beatniks but now called peace-nicks."

I got up on stage in front of all the coffee tables, and I was ready to read my poem. When they saw my uniform and realized that I was in the military, the room went so quiet. You could hear a *pin drop!*

I spoke into the mike, "Hello, I'm Stuart. *I'd like to read you a poem. Here goes!*"

War sucks! Not good.
War sucks. Not good.

War sucks! Not good.
*Let's take our clothes off and
dance around.
That's more fun!
Thank you!*

When I sat down, they all cheered! *They
loved it!*

Joanie kissed me, got up, and said, *"That
was great, Stuart!"*

"I've got to go now. Nice meeting you."

Outside, I saw that Joanie was given one
of those "tickets," or whatever it was, that the
costume people across the street had. I saw
them talking. *Joanie pointed me out to them
while I was looking out the window.* I needed
to go too, but I didn't know where. I had no
plans.

When I got out, I looked around at *lots of
interesting-looking people. I was the only one
in a sailor suit.* Then, the two strangely dressed
people came over to speak to me. "Joanie
says you are a performer, *and* even if you are
not, *you look interesting to us! We are inviting
you to a very exclusive private party—by invitation only! Now if you take this invitation, do not
give it to anyone else! It's for your eyes only!"*

I said, "Okay." I gave it back. "I'd like to go,
but I am new around here. And *I'd never find
the party!"*

126

"Okay," they said, "you can follow us there!"

Inside the "invitation only" exclusive party, it was dark with multicolored strobe lights and loud live music playing. A half-naked lady with blue hair and *very firm pointed boobs grabbed my hands.* She wore purple "pasties" with tassels. She showed her talent by *twirling the tassels.* "I'm Nancy, and this is my boyfriend Brian," she said.

"Hi, Nancy," I replied.

Nancy sat on one side of me, while Brian sat on the other. Nancy had a drink in her hand. "Would you like to drink this, Stuart?" she said with a big smile.

"Of course, I do!" I said and gulped it down. Soon I was *buzzed* on alcohol. Nancy had her arm around me and kissed me *in front of her boyfriend Brian.* Then she was smoking something. "Stuart, do you want to try this?"

"I don't smoke," I said.

She kissed me on the mouth and put my hands on her boobs. "Sure you don't want to smoke this?"

"Of *course,* I do!" I said.

Nancy and I smoked it. Nancy French-kissed me—her tongue inside my mouth. Then Nancy handed me a pill. "Stuart, do you want to take this pill?"

"Of *course,* I do, Nancy!" I answered.

Stuart Is Stoned Now

I was more relaxed than ever before. Everything was dreamlike. I saw colors and felt wonderful. Noises were louder, and I heard voices and music in my head. I was floating in air. "This is great! Wow!" I was thinking, *If I don't die tonight, I've got to try this again someday!*

I blacked out and didn't remember *any-thing* of what happened next the night before. But I woke up to music of Trini Lopez, singing "Lemon Tree, Very Pretty."

I was in *someone's bed! I didn't have any pants on!* Then I heard someone in the kitchen. It was Brian!

"Hey, where are my pants?" I asked.

Brian said, "You threw up on them! We had them dry-cleaned for you!" Brian handed me my Navy blue uniform—all cleaned and pressed.

"Thanks, Brian! I'll be leaving now." As I left, Nancy came out of another room and gave me a thank-you note. It read, "Thanks for com-ing to my party. Love, Andy."

Who's Andy? I wondered.

"Goodbye," they both said.

All my money was still in my wallet.

As I walked to the bus station, I had a hang-over, but I also had a feeling of being a deflated tire. I caught the next bus back to New Jersey as quickly as I could. Now, there was no doubt in my mind that *I wanted to go home. I was ready to go to college now.*

Stuart is twenty-one now. His dependency on alcohol and drugs began to increase.

CHAPTER TWELVE

Owl Junior College Daze

Back at my parents' home in New Jersey, I was thinking about getting ready to take a scary step forward and attempt to go to college. I was already a high school dropout, but I had the US Navy and the GI Bill funding ready today for my college expenses. But I couldn't get *Bonnie* off my mind! As I sipped on my daily alcoholic beverage that day and brought the glass to my lips, I wondered what went wrong. *I almost had a wife, and I somehow blew it. She got away and married someone else. Why didn't Bonnie wait for me? I* promised *her that I'd see her before she turned twenty-four.* I was still obsessed with thoughts of her about ten months after Bonnie had left back to Scotland.

I got a phone call from Aunt Judy. I learned something else—news from Scotland about Bonnie that sent me into *more heavy alcoholic drinking. Bonnie had a son now!* She and her husband Jimmy had a baby boy! *It's none of my business. It very well could be her husband's son, and* Bonnie is happy now. I knew I needed to *let it go* now and live my own life, *but when I drank alcohol, which was daily, the Bonnie obsession returned in full force. I just couldn't forget her.*

My cat Sparky sat on my bed, which now was on a screened-in porch converted into a guestroom in my parents' "new" home in Eastfield, New Jersey.

I was earning money, doing odd jobs around the neighborhood, such as painting and mowing people's lawns using my father's old hand-pushed mower in my neighborhood. One morning, a couple of houses down from mine, I saw our neighbor, *State Senator Harry Jones* himself, out in his huge front lawn with a nice new mower, mowing his *own* front lawn! The senator was usually busy in Washington DC. I'd only seen him a couple of times before, and that was when he was mowing. The "good senator" was a down-to-earth guy like me.

So this day, I had a beer for breakfast and had the Dutch courage to walk up to the senator and ask him, "Good morning, Senator. *Can I mow your lawn this morning?*"

Senator Harry Jones suddenly looked very happy. "Sure, son! Use my mower! I'll pay you well!"

"Thanks a lot for helping me out, giving me this job, Senator. You've got *my vote!*"

"*Thank you!*" he said to me. And he paid me *pretty good money* just for mowing the lawn. He left $100 cash under his back door floor mat. *He was a good man!* I made up my mind to go register to vote, and I did, so I could vote for honest men in government, like my good neighbor, Senator Harry Jones. He not only drank alcohol with me, he provided it—only the *very best!* Stuart and Senator Harry

Jones were both alcoholics and became drinking buddies for a few months.

And I spent nearly all of my money on, what else, alcohol. I became a recluse and did not go out of my porch room much except to mow a few lawns to have *more* money to buy alcohol. I was *sad* and *depressed*, thinking and obsessing over my lost loves overseas in Scotland and Ireland. It was all about "*Poor me, pour me a drink!*"

Yes, indeed, I was a *daily drinker* now. Both my parents still worked, and I was still a *latchkey kid*, wandering around unattended without any direction in my life. Only now I was twenty-one years old, and I was an *adult*.

Drunk One More Time

I decided right then and there that when I turned twenty-four years of age, even if I did not finish college or even started it, that I *would* return to Scotland and visit Bonnie before she turned twenty-four.

"Why?" I reasoned with myself, "Because *I promised her* and said *I would see her* before she was twenty-four years old." And even deeper than that was yet *another* reason. *What if Bonnie's son* was really my son? *I am a man of honor, and I keep my word. Yes, I* would *still marry her if she* needed *me to*. At the same time, I knew nothing happened at all when I was drunk.

By now, I had switched from drinking scotch to drinking brandy and sometimes rum, like I used to drink in Jamaica.

As I lift the glass of alcohol to my lips, I wondered, *Why can't I be like other people? Why can't I find someone to marry? Other people seem to have it all together, while I am without direction and purpose in my life. Such a deep mystery!* I pondered.

I came up with a *plan*. I had failed high school, but while in the US Navy, I did pass the GED, the high school general equivalency diploma test, when I was only seventeen. I could use that GED to get into a junior college. Then, after I finished a two-year junior college, I would go see Bonnie. That was my plan.

I was accepted into *Owl Junior College* in Cranberry, New Jersey. I bought my first car and drove to college. It was spring of 1968 at Owl Junior College. Owl Junior College *was not at all what I had expected. All the students were talking about was the war in Vietnam and about the civil rights movement and even women's rights!*

I was out of the US Navy now. I had my *honorable discharge! I was very proud of having served my country!*

Instead of studying, people were saying to one another, "Which side are you on?"

Then some were asking me *which side I was on?*

"*What do you mean?*" I asked.

"Are you a *dove* or a *hawk?*" they asked me. They were singing protest songs, like the ones of years ago that I heard Joanie sing in the coffee house in the village.

Between my basic math class and beginning Spanish class, I saw in the college hallways some US Marines come in dressed in "dress" uniforms. They set up a marine recruitment stand-up display and set up a table with literature. Their intent was to recruit new students to go join the marines to go right into the *Vietnam War.*

Surprise! Then, I saw something else right next to the marine recruitment table, *something shocking to me at the time—a confrontation! Another table* was set up right next to the marines by the students. This table had "anti-war" *protest literature about the Vietnam War on it!*

Standing behind the students' counter (I was not sure I believed it) were three students wearing full dress *military uniforms!* The US Army, Air Force, and Marines were represented but *no Navy.* One student in an Air Force blue uniform and the student protest anti-war *leader himself* was wearing a full-dress *marine sergeant's uniform!* It was *all military student veterans running and leading the anti-war table! Unbelievable!*

They had convincing, well-written literature on the table, including a newspaper that said, *"Vietnam veterans against the war!"*

I read it, and it even had four-star generals in the paper stating their views against the Vietnam War!

And also, mingled in with the veterans at the anti-war table were, of course, pretty college coeds. They were asking people to *join* their college protest group. *Owl Junior College* had its own student newspaper, and I was already on its staff. But this group also had its own paper: an *underground, unofficial newspaper!* The group called itself "NAPALM: Now Association for a Peaceful American Liberal Movement."

One of the coeds behind the table looked at me and said, "Hi, I'm *Sharon.* You must be new around here. *I did not see you last fall."*

"You are right, Sharon," I answered. "I just started here this spring. I was in the military too," I said.

"Really? What branch?" Sharon asked.

"The US Navy," I replied.

Sharon smiles. "Come with me!"

Sharon excitedly grabbed the student protest leader wearing the marine sergeant's uniform. "Hey, Lenny!" Sharon said. "We have veterans from *all* branches of the service *now!"*

"What do you mean, sweetheart?" Lenny asked Sharon.

"Stuart here is a US Navy veteran! And he wants to join us!" Sharon said.

I do? I was thinking.

"Welcome to NAPALM, sailor! *We need you, Stuart!"* Lenny said.

And at that moment, *I needed a drink!* I went home that day with a bunch of peace literature.

Soon, it was the winter quarter semester of 1968 already at Owl College. My grades so far were Cs, Ds, and one B for the first two quarter semesters. It was difficult, but I was trying. But before I knew it, *I was being transformed* into a "hippie" myself. My hair grew long, and I grew a beard.

I helped write anti-war articles for the NAPALM <u>and</u> the student newspaper. Soon, even the newspaper *Vietnam Veterans Against the War* had a protest article in it, written by me in it, that was *reprinted* from the underground NAPALM student protest newspaper.

Also, at Owl College, civil rights was an issue. So Lenny and I helped start the "Gray Club" for *black and white equality.* The Beatles came out in 1968 with the *White Album* with songs on it like "Revolution," "Helter Skelter," and "Why Don't We Do It in the Road." John Lennon was active in the San Francisco peace movement.

I hung around Sharon's place, and she gave me things that "took me away" in my mind. We played "Lucy in the Sky with Diamonds" by the Beatles and got high.

Sharon's place was a small studio apartment near Owl College. She burned incense, and it is always dark in her room. She was Lenny's girlfriend. Because Sharon also supported "women's rights," she never wore a bra or panties. I was drinking a beer on the sofa; and Sharon came on to me, kissing me, saying, *"Let's make love, man!"* She said that it would be *really groovy!* She was getting *high* and smoking something.

"That's heavy!" I said.

"Why so heavy?" she asked.

"Because you are *Lenny's* girl!" I explained.

"Man, we have an open relationship," she answered. "We *make love to whomever we want to! Free love, Stuart!"*

"Groovy, man," I said.

"Well, come on then," she said. "Let's make love!"

"Sorry, Sharon, I can't—still *heavy!"*

"Oh," she said, "I'm sorry, maybe you like guys!"

"No, Sharon...it's not that."

"Well, what then?" she asked.

Stuart Too Drunk to Do Anything

"I'm saving myself for *my wife!"* I told her.

"*Wow!*" Sharon said as she took another puff on her smoke. "*That's heavy!* Sorry, I did not know you were married."

"I'm not married."

"Okay, we can be friends."

"Groovy," I said.

Sharon took off all her clothes and lay on top of Stuart. He was drunk as he kissed her all over and passed out.

And I was a heavy beer drinker too now, having switched over from hard liquor to beer and "whatever else" Sharon had. I was drunk and loaded almost all the time. *I forgot about going to classes or doing homework at Owl College.*

Once again, the college protest group NAPALM rented a bus. Anyone from Owl College who wanted to could go with us to a "protest rally" in New York City to Central Park.

As I drove my car, I visited my mom that Saturday morning before catching the student protest bus. My mom said to me, "Don't forget to bring a rag or something to wipe *the blood off.*"

There had been a lot of news about the police beating up war protestors. Sharon carried a bunch of signs that said Make Love Not War!

When we arrived at the Central Park protest rally, I was dressed with long hair, a beard, beads, and colorful clothes, and, of course, *bell-bottom sailor pants.*

I carried a sign with the peace symbol on top which I held high. It said Ban the Bomb. It was identical to the sign that the protestors back in Scotland had. Only I was carrying it now! I still had guilty feelings about loading Polaris missiles that could kill millions of people.

In New York City's *Central Park*, it was a festive occasion—a *sea of protestors* singing "Give Peace a Chance." And up from a two-story apartment window was the sound of a loudspeaker in the window playing more protest songs like Sweetwater, singing "Motherless Child," and Country Joe and the Fish singing "The Fixin' to Die Rag," and "We Shall Overcome."

> One, two, three, four,
> What are we fighting for?
> Don't know, and don't give a
> damn...
> Going off to Vietnam...
> Be the first one on your block
> To have your kid come home
> in a box!"

Wow, what a song! But this next one was more to the point:

> Please don't drop that
> H-bomb *on me.*
> You can drop it *on yourself!*

Playing everywhere in Central Park were lots of good songs on the loudspeaker. Bob Dylan and Joan Baez's songs were very good. But Joan Baez reminded me of "someone."

Nah...it couldn't be, I thought to myself.

The afternoon's main event were celebrity speakers, including Coretta King. In the end, it was a peaceful protest—a lovely day—except for one far corner of the park, where a small fight occurred, and of course that made front page news.

The afternoon at Central Park ended when the park police tried to tell the protestors to "Go home!" Some did not want to leave, so they did a "sit-in" and sat around on the ground while shouting the anti-war slogan: *"Hell no! We won't go!"*

The newspapers and television stations did not show much of our "peaceful side" but instead showed the police dragging away these protestors—students—to *paddy wagons!*

"Another example of *yellow journalism* by the establishment," said Lenny.

As the year 1968 came to an end, a lot had happened. First, "Eugene McCarthy for President" got the students' support, then support went to Robert Kennedy. He was assassinated, and then Martin Luther King was also killed. NAPALM had a bus ready to go to the Chicago convention, but Senator Eugene McCarthy in a news story told students to stay home. And all of us did, except for Lenny and Sharon. At the end of 1968, the US landed on the moon. But really, *I didn't remember much of 1968. I was drunk and loaded for most of it!*

CHAPTER THIRTEEN

The Search

Lifting a glass of whiskey to my lips, I wondered *why* I flunked out of college! It was a big mystery to me. My grades at Owl College did *not* get above Ds and Fs mostly because I was too involved in the hectic days of the 1968 Peace Movement, and I did not bother to attend classes.

"Hey, Stuart, maybe it's your drinking alcohol," a voice said.

I decided to try to find employment. I got a good job in a factory that manufactured truck mirrors—very large flat sideview mirrors to be installed on each side of a truck cab and truck lights for big rig trucks, Detroit Dinosaurs.

I was hired as the catalog and mail room department manager. What I did was mail out new product flyers, catalogs, and advertisements to auto and truck supply stores all over the United States and the world.

The vice president of sales named Randy was the man who hired me. He drove a *brand-*

new *Cadillac*. Every year, he got a *new one*. When I ran errands for this company, Randy would give me the keys to his new Cadillac for me to drive around.

Stuart's Beer Can Apartment

I moved out my parents' house and got myself a studio apartment. Soon, *all the walls of the apartment were lined with beer cans* from floor to ceiling.

Detroit Dinosaur Mirror Company, the truck company where I was employed, had *two factories*: one in New Jersey and the other in Brooklyn, New York.

Soon I had a regular income, and *I was twenty-four years old*. I remembered the "promise" that I made to Bonnie. I needed closure. And I wanted to see if she was happy and if that guy, her husband Jimmy, was treating her right.

Because of my company's policy, I accumulated vacation time off. So I got a *passport* to go back to Scotland to see what happened to my lost love Bonnie. I was determined to say my "goodbyes" to Bonnie. I wrote a letter to Bonnie's parents, telling them, "I'll be in Scotland next Saturday, and I'll be driving up the road to their door in Scotland at 10:00 a.m."

Having driven my boss's brand-new luxury Cadillac around, with my airplane ticket to Scotland, I paid in advance for the *most expensive luxury car I could rent* at the airport to try to make Bonnie think that I was a *successful businessman*. I was a drunken nobody, but I did not want Bonnie to know that. And I was there on a business trip—*personal business!* I needed closure.

The flight to Scotland was Friday night. I got on the airplane at Newark, New Jersey Airport, and it was a six-hour airplane ride across the Atlantic. I was afraid of heights and flying, so I asked the stewardess to bring me "one" drink.

Soon, Stuart was wasted—drunk as a skunk! After a six-hour flight over the Atlantic Ocean, my plane finally landed safely in Scotland. It was 3:00 a.m. on my watch.

I had an alcoholic hangover. And because I had a fear of heights, *I was drunk, but I could not sleep at all* on that airplane. Stuart had a fear of crashing.

Most days in Scotland, it was raining, but on this Saturday morning, the *sun* was out. *I forgot about the time change*—six hours ahead! *It was already 9:00 a.m. in Scotland!*

I was a mess! My fancy suit that I wore on the plane was all wrinkled up! My luxury car was waiting. I grabbed a cup of Scottish coffee and looked at maps so I know how to drive to Bonnie's house. I was still disoriented from drinking on the plane. My head was fuzzy with a hangover.

I climbed into my brand-new rental *luxury car*, and right away, I noticed *something was not right about this! The steering wheel of the car was wrong! It was mounted on the right side of the dashboard, not on the left side as in the USA!*

In a hurry, I needed to go because if Bonnie was at her parents' house waiting, I didn't want to be late! What if she *did not believe I was really coming?* I must show Bonnie that *I kept my word—I was a man of integrity!*

Okay, very soon, I got used to *sitting on the right side of the front seat.* I had never driven a car while I was in Scotland or never even rode in a Scottish car, except taxis. Before, I had always taken a double-decker red bus or the train.

As I headed out the Scottish airport, I noticed another *strange thing: All the cars were driving on the* wrong *side of the road!* In Scotland, you drove on the left side of the road!

My watch said 3:30 a.m. now, which was 9:30 a.m. in Scotland.

As I stepped on the gas heading out the airport, I was *confused* at first about driving. *Should I be on the left side of the road or the right side?* So I drove *in the middle! Boom.* I smashed the whole side of the new luxury car against a steel post as I exited the airport. I got out to take a look. The whole left side was dented! I kept going! I had to get to Bonnie's house! Now, instead of me showing off with driving a luxury car, *I had to hide the car!*

Traffic was good. I was driving okay, but to me, it was still on the wrong side of the road. I arrived at Bonnie's old street. I parked my smashed-up luxury car *way down the hill* on the bottom of her road and walked up to Bonnie's parents' house.

Wow, I made it! It was *five minutes before 10:00 a.m.!* I was at *Bonnie's old house!*

I'm here! I thought.

Stuart Drinks Six Beers

I knew Bonnie was twenty-three years old now. I was keeping my promise that I would return before she was twenty-four. I knocked. Bonnie's father answered the door. "Oh! *Bonnie is not home.* We were expecting you."

"*Not home?*" I said. "Well, I am here in Scotland on *a business trip.* I just *happened* to be *passing through* this way, and I just wanted to say *hello* to everyone!

"Good to see you again, Stuart!" said Bonnie's dad.

Just then, another luxury car, even better than my rental, pulled up and parked in front.

Oh my god! It's Bonnie!

Bonnie got out of the car and so did another man. "Good to see you again, Stuart," Bonnie said. "This is *my husband, Jimmy.* Our son went out to play with his friend. He will be back later. Come inside so we can talk."

"Just a moment, Bonnie...I need to run down to the corner shop for a second," I replied. *"I'll be right back!"*

My dented car was in front of the shop. *I could see that Bonnie was happy and that Jimmy was a nice guy.* I got a bag of gifts out my car and brought it up to the house where Bonnie was.

She opened the door. "Come on in," she said.

"I've really got to run, Bonnie. I brought these gifts for your family and also a belated wedding gift for you too. I must hurry along because I have a business meeting to get to. Bye, Bonnie."

"Cheerio." Bonnie waved goodbye as I walked along down the road. *"Nice car you have, Stuart!"* she yelled.

The wedding gift I gave them was a *bottle of Jack Daniels whiskey.* I was heartbroken but happy that Bonnie was okay. I could move on now.

More Demoralization

I drove the rental car to Glasgow. It was so easy by car to get there and fast. I could hardly believe it. I had six days of vacation left. I returned the rental car at Glasgow Train Station and caught a train to England.

I had a camera and snapped a photo of myself under a tall clock tower named "Big Ben" in London. I had a passport, so next, I took an overnight boat ride from the Isle of Wright to Belgium. I rented another car, a BMW, and drove to Germany, then Denmark, and then to Holland.

As I parked in *Holland*, I noticed *canals of water with storefront windows*, like in USA department stores only this was *way* different because "live women" *were inside the display windows just sitting there*! It was night.

In Holland, *prostitution was legal*. So I got more drunk. I was looking at the window displays, checking out the ladies, and at the *very tall apartments* all around the lighted canals. Then, *I noticed something*! I remembered my job as a catalog department manager! Wow!

Detroit Dinosaur Company's truck mirrors were mounted outside on all of the apartment building's windows! Wow! That was our mirrors up there, all right!

"That's a model 1203!" I shouted. Another one of *our mirrors*, a 1800 series truck mirror over there, was attached to a building on the third floor window! I'd recognize those mirrors anywhere! Even in Holland on a building!

I was really drunk, stumbling around in my tourist clothes with a camera. Suddenly a lady pulled me aside and led me into a small dark room. I had just bought a souvenir leather wallet with a *windmill* on it, and *her dog* was chewing on it!

I asked the lady, "What are *my* truck mirrors doing up on the windows?"

The lady explained, "So working ladies can see if we have *any customers coming*!"

"Thanks, lady," I said and drank a bottle of dutch whiskey.

I blacked out, which meant I didn't remember what happened next, but I woke up the next morning, sleeping in my rental BMW car!

By next Monday, I was back in the USA and back in New Jersey and back at work. *But finally, I had closure on Bonnie.* I could let her go now and move on.

Now, I would search for the right woman to be my wife. But where was she?

CHAPTER FOURTEEN

The Choice

Stuart Searches for His True Love

Another year went by since closure with Bonnie. Stuart will tell you what happened next.

My father suggested that since I was *still not amounting to anything, I was a college drop-out and a drunk, that maybe I could marry a rich lady from a well-to-do family*—find some lady from a family that *he would approve of!*

Then, my father told me, "Stuart, *here is what I suggest. First, find at least three women who want to marry you.* After you have selected at least three that *you* want to marry, tell them all about one another and see what they do! You can try any one of those match-making services."

"Okay, Dad...I'll try it," I said.

I began checking out "marriage-minded" pen pal sites, "mail-order brides," and "match-making services." I wanted to find a good wife.

After a while, drinking my *tenth* beer today, I was *sure* that if I only got married *to the right woman*, my life would be normal. I'd be happy then. I could still drink alcohol then.

I paid a $300 deposit to *Maxine's Matches*, which specialized in matching wealthy women with husbands. But first, I had to go in for a *personal interview with Maxine herself* in New York City.

Before too long, I was inside Maxine's office for her personal interview. I told Maxine that I was the manager of a catalog distribution center. (That was one way of saying catalog department manager.) Then Maxine, the matchmaker, looked out her office window to *check out what kind of car I was driving*! She saw a shiny new Cadillac.

This day, I was near Maxine's office, in New York City anyway, because I was running errands for my company at our Brooklyn office and happened to be driving the vice president's, Randy's, *new car*.

Maxine looked and saw his *brand-new Cadillac* parked in the visitor's lot. *She thought it was my car!*

"Mr. Stuart," she said, "I looked over your paperwork, and I think I have the *perfect match for you*! Her name was Rhoda. She lived in Fort Lee, New Jersey. She was Jewish, and you are Unitarian. Your interests seem the same."

"What do you mean?" I said.

"You *both* want someone to *marry!* So that means...you're a match."

"*Ohh,* okay, sounds good. I'll *pick her!*" I said.

Maxine set us up with a date.

I drove to Fort Lee, New Jersey, to some luxury high-rise apartments overlooking the George Washington Bridge and the New York City skyline. Rhoda was on the top floor. I met her and her family. *They were all checking me out!* Her father was an Orthodox Jewish man. I was invited for dinner. I was shy, but some Manischewitz wine soon gave me the Dutch courage I needed to talk to them. I drank the whole bottle! I had no idea what I said. But Rhoda liked me, and I liked her.

We hardly got any time to be alone; but as I left Rhoda's apartment, she pulled me close to her and kissed me and looked into my eyes and said, "*Stuart, you seem much nicer than those other guys. Maybe you and I are a marriage match!*"

"I feel that way about you too, Rhoda."

She said, "I paid good money for this match."

She was very pretty. And I wondered what was under her clothes. Before too long, I did find out! Rhoda wanted to be sure that we were compatible in bed. She had come prepared with *condoms* in her purse and a bottle of Manischewitz!

"Shouldn't we wait until we marry?" I asked.

I drank her wine, then I passed out on the floor. One down, two more to go!

When the second one, Good World Match Maker Service for Wealthy Women, called me for an interview, I was not sure what to tell them. When they interviewed me over the phone, instead of answering their questions, I told them, "Well, I've *already found a marriage prospect from Maxine's Matches*."

"Oh!" they said. "If you are already a *client* of *Maxine*, you qualify with us too! We are worldwide, you know, and we have a lovely lady who is a *perfect match for you!*"

"Where does she live?" I asked.

"Casablanca, Morocco!"

I got the lovely lady's address, and Good World Matchmaker Service informed "Melody" that she found the right man *for her*.

I asked, "How do you know we are the right match for each other?"

"You are *single* and a *gentleman!* She *will want to marry you. Trust me!*"

I looked at her photo. She was *very pretty!* I guess professional matchmakers *really knew what they were doing!*

Two down. Find one more lady first to marry.

The dates with Rhoda were fun! We got along well, and *nice letters and photos came from my lady, Melody, in Casablanca.* I was excited! Which lady would it be?

Then, out of the blue, I got some mail from a *marriage-minded pen pal service in Mexico* of all places! I opened it up, and it had lots of ladies' photos in there—black-and-white pictures. Hundreds of pretty ladies all saying they were "marriage-minded." In this month's issue on the twentieth page on the left bottom corner, I saw a photo of a *beautiful Mexican maiden. A warm glow came over me.*

I think that's her! I don't know why. It's love at first sight from a photo! "Get a grip, Stuart," I said to myself. "The catalog is probably old photos, and she most likely has found someone else."

The lady's address in Mexico would be given to me if I sent money. So I sent for it. Soon, I wrote to Maria and sent her a photo of me and my cat Sparky. I forgot all about it until one day, I got a letter from Mexico with *more* pictures of Maria. She was gorgeous! Long black hair, *beautiful,* with enchanting eyes—the *prettiest girl I ever laid eyes on. Bonnie who?* I was in love with Maria now, and I *hoped* she was the one. But there was *one more thing I had to do!*

Stuart then remembered what his father told him: find three ladies to marry, then *tell them all about one another and see what they do.*

Here was what I did. First, I told Rhoda. I called her up. "Rhoda, marriage is a big step. I need to tell you *I am considering you for marriage*, but I also have two other women I am considering for marriage. I am trying to decide who to choose!"

Rhoda replied, "Make up your mind, Stuart, soon! I don't want to be wasting my time!

Next, I wrote the pretty lady, Melody, in Casablanca, and told her the same message!

"Just let me know what you decide, Stuart," she said. "I *hope* you choose *me!*"

One more lady to tell—Maria. I was thinking and worrying, *Maybe I'll lose all of them and have no one to marry! Why does my father think this is a good idea? Oh, well...here goes. I will tell Maria the message.*

So I wrote Maria and told her,

> Maria, marriage is a *big decision*. I need to tell you I am considering *you for marriage* but also have *two other women I am also considering*. I am trying to decide who to choose."

Maria answered me,

> "Stuart, if you decide to marry someone else, I will be *very sad,* but *I also will be happy to know that you are happy!*"

Good answer! Maria was my choice!
I wrote Maria back.

It is *you*, Maria, that I choose.

I knew before this *instinctively* God had answered my prayer. Maria was the right woman, and it came to pass that when we met in person, *we instantly fell in love!*

Stuart has found his true love. Would he be happy now? Not a chance! Alcohol and drug addiction gets worse over time.

CHAPTER FIFTEEN

Happy Daze in Mexico

Stuart Goes to Mexico

While drinking my third six-pack beer, I was getting ready to go to Mexico, *not as a tourist*, bringing back a sombrero or Mexican blanket. *No, not me*. I was going to Mexico *on a mission: to come back with a beautiful senorita as my wife. And her name was Maria.*

I was sure if I got married and had a family, then everything in my life would be normal and fine—happy forever after.

Daily drinking of alcohol was normal for me now. I was not really happy with my choices in the past, and *more drinking helped me forget everything and everybody.* But when I sobered up, *the problems were worse. But* happiness was waiting for me right around the corner of my life, and *Maria was my destiny.*

May 1971

My airplane left Newark, New Jersey, airport; went to Dallas, Texas, with a transfer to a *Mexican Airlines* flight. I stopped at Dallas Airport to get a haircut so I would look nice. I bought some postcards and a *Humorous Easy—Learn to Speak It* Spanish-English picture dictionary at the airport gift shop. I almost forgot I could not speak a word of Spanish. I flunked Spanish class at Owl College, and *Maria did not speak any English—not a word!* When Maria's letters came, I had paid someone to translate them into English.

As I was boarding the Mexican Airlines flight heading for Guadalajara, Mexico, I thought, *How exciting and adventurous this is!* But more exciting was the fact that I knew *Maria would meet me at the airport!*

I was nervous! I'm scared. I was on an airplane! My desire for Maria overcame my fear of heights. So motivated by the prospect of true love at last and romance, at least for one day, I was not picking up that first drink, even on the plane. I could drink after I met her.

I was using beat-up looking suitcases because I didn't want to look like a "tourist," but I did anyway because I was one. I looked and acted like a fish out of water because the *contrast* from New Jersey to downtown Guadalajara, Mexico, seemed to me like I landed on *another planet!* Everything was *new, strange, and totally different* than the life I knew—trumpet music playing happy Mexican songs; Mariachis walking around singing, playing guitars; *live animals and exotic birds in cages for sale in the marketplace*; people all around me trying to *beg for money*; and street performers, such as *fire-eaters and jugglers.*

I was lost, and I must look like it. There were buses and trucks and cars outside the airport. Finally and magically, I looked into the distance. I could see through a passing bus's pollution of black smoke rising in the air someone coming my way. I could instinctively tell. *It was Maria!*

And it was her! She looked like an *angel* coming through the fog to save me, and there she was. She took me by the hand and led me to a quiet park. She had another lady with her tor company, her niece, who lived in Guadalajara. Soon, Maria communicated to me somehow and explained to me that she did *not live near Guadalajara* and that we had to get on a bus and ride for four more hours to get to where she lived.

The good thing was that it was love at first sight, but more than that, I could tell that she was a *lady of quality*. She had a very rare "presence" about her, and she was smart, kind, and loving. And next, as the "big test," I tried to make romantic advances toward her as much as I could, but I could not get past a kiss. And it sounded like her translation was *"no ringy, no thingy."* And she pointed to her ring finger, making it clear *we would have to be married first*! That was exactly the kind of woman Stuart was looking for.

We had a couple of hours before the bus ride, and we went to a park *and a zoo*. I needed to talk, so I got out my Spanish-English translation book and *read exactly* a phrase from this book written in Spanish.

At the zoo in front of a gorilla cage, I asked Maria in Spanish something directly from my translation book: "Do you have any gorillas in your house?" That was exactly what my book said. *She looks surprised*. She took my book and read it and wrote something. I tried to translate it into English, and I thought she wrote "Not before, but I do now—*you!*"

We had lots of laughs on the long dark bus ride. It was a happy four hours, holding Maria sleeping in my arms, both of us thinking of *happy days* together ahead.

Stuart Remembers a Train Ride in Scotland

Then, I remembered long ago in my Navy days riding the train in Scotland that man with the turban who got married *out of curiosity.* He *said he had a good wife.* That was what I prayed for, and that was all I'd ever wanted.

When we arrived at the little Mexican village where Maria lived, it was midnight and dark. Maria communicated with me that she was *leaving me and going home!* It was dark. She had a taxi waiting for her but took me too. The taxi was playing loud Mexican music. She dropped me off in the center of the little town at a hotel. Maria said, "Go in, gorilla, and because you are my guest, *the hotel is already paid for!*"

It seemed like five minutes later, morning arrived in Mexico by the sound of roosters crowing at the break of dawn. I discovered I was in Tepic, Nayarit, Mexico. It was 1971. I looked around my hotel room and out my window to a busy dirt street and women walking around with baskets balanced on their heads and the sounds of cats meowing in the distance and dogs barking.

I walked around a little. A huge cutout sign of cartoon Lulu was hanging on the next building. And in this strange town (to me), I wondered where Maria was. But she soon came to my rescue and took me to another place to stay. They were like apartments with a center courtyard in the middle. Very nice. Maria said I could stay there at *no charge*. Her aunt owned the place.

Soon, Maria took me to meet her mother, who was a very nice person. She had been a good example to Maria. The place I was staying at seemed to have professional people and college students living there, including an American exchange student by the name of Harold. *Wow, another American who speaks English!*

I wanted to pop the big question to Maria, but she did not speak English. I didn't speak Spanish, but my gut feeling was that she was the woman God had chosen for me.

After small talk with Harold, I told him, "I'm here to marry Maria. As *one American to another, tell me the truth* and what you know about her. And do you think I'd be making a wise choice to have Maria as my wife?"

Harold looked at me with a very serious look, right in the eyes. "Well, Maria works at a bank. I've never seen her cavorting with any men. She is always polite and kind. So *now*, I *will give you my honest opinion.* Stuart, from all I have observed and know about her..."

"Well, *what, Harold*?"

"Stuart, you would be *crazy* and a complete *idiot* and *fool not to marry her*! You won't find a better woman anywhere!"

"Thanks, Harold," I said. "I *already knew that*!"

Stuart knew then Maria was the choice.

Before I had left New Jersey, my mother had given me a credit card to use only in emergencies. My cash money was almost gone. I bought an engagement ring and wedding ring, and that very same afternoon, I proposed marriage to Maria, on my knees, of course.

I asked her, "Will you marry me, Maria?"

She said, "Si!"

And we both jumped up and down, kissed, and we were happy and excited.

Then, Harold came to me and told me, "*Congratulations!*"

At this point I have been drinking Mexican *cerveza* (beer) daily and tequila.

"What have I done? I'm getting married. And before I leave Mexico, I want Maria to become my wife."

Harold told me something else, "Not so fast, buddy! Before you can marry Maria, *you have to get permission to do so from the Mexican government.*"

"I do? What does that mean?" I asked as I drank another beer.

"You need to travel to Mexico City to an office that specializes in Americans and others who want to get married to Mexican citizens. Maria has relatives in Mexico City who will meet you there and show you where to go. After your airplane to Mexico City lands, go to a small hotel, the Sombrero Hotel, that Maria's family has paid for. It's easy to find because it's near a big hotel called the Havana Hotel. The next morning, Maria's relatives will pick you up. Here is their phone number."

Harold handed me the information.

That night, I had to fly from Guadalajara to Mexico City. I hoped the wings didn't fall off. I needed some alcohol to drink. Flying was still scary, and I had a fear of heights. But when Stuart was drunk, he had no fear.

When the plane landed in Mexico City in the late afternoon, I had a hangover. I went to get my beat-up-looking suitcase from the airport baggage claim and headed for my hotel. I was tired.

I saw the Sombrero Hotel off in the distance. As I came closer to the building, I thought I was going into the lobby of the right hotel, but it was the lobby of *Hotel Havana*! I had a red, white, and blue shirt on, and I did look like an American tourist because I was one, or sorts.

I checked in. All the Havana Hotel staff looked me over. I still thought that I was in the Sombrero Hotel. I was not sure what my hosts thought. Maybe I was a spy for them. America was still in a cold war with Cuba, but I got a *warm and friendly welcome* from the Hotel Havana manager. My shirt had an American flag on the back.

"Welcome to Hotel Havana! *We have been expecting you, sir, and we have the best room for you at no charge.*"

"Thanks," I said. "I'm very tired."

The next morning, I heard roosters crowing even in downtown Mexico City. Upon awakening sober, I suddenly realized I was in the wrong hotel, and I phoned Maria's relatives. Luckily, they spoke English.

I packed my suitcase and left the Havana Hotel. "You've done good. I'll put in a good word for you," I said as I went out the door. I was happy to get out of there. But in fairness, I turned around, and I went back in there and *paid for the room*. "I'm just a tourist," I explained. "Thanks, you have a good hotel."

Soon, a man came up to me who had blond hair and blue eyes. "I am Maria's cousin."

Soon, I was in a whole family of Mexican-German citizens with blond hair. They let me stay at their house and were very nice to me. They showed me where the office was where I needed to get the Mexican Government's permission. Next day, I waited for *five hours* in an office, and finally, an office clerk interviewed me and looked over my paperwork and my passport! Then he said, "*You are approved!* Go pick up your permission papers *tomorrow* at 2:00 p.m. inside *Revolution Hall*."

"Okay, thanks," I said.

At 2:00 p.m., I was there on time, and to my surprise, two thousand other guys were also inside Revolution Hall that day. Finally, over the loudspeaker, the voice asked, "Who here is getting permission to marry a Mexican lady?" I could not believe it!

"We all are!" they said in unison.

I took a bus to Tepic from Mexico City. It was a sixteen-hour bus ride—hot dusty open windows on the bus, chickens on the bus, beggars at bus stops, no toilet paper or even toilet seats in some of the rest stops.

As the bus motor purred along with an occasional backfire (bang), I tried to relax as well as I could in my hard bus seat. I was happy knowing that I had the official paperwork that I needed to marry Maria. I had plenty of chances to "chicken out." I even had two backup addresses in Mexico in case Maria did not work out. Even on that long final bus ride, a pretty señorita had her eye on me. So did her mom and tried to speak to me.

I told her, "I wish I could get to know you, but I have a fiancée already. And I'm on my way to marry her."

The señorita then went to talk to some other guy on the bus.

Back in Tepic, Maria was glad that I did not run away, and so was I. But I was insecure and drank some more margaritas. Wedding arrangements had been made for us by Maria's family.

Harold told me, "Well, my friend, you have to have a *civil wedding first* then a *formal wedding the next day!*"

Wow, I thought, *I get to marry Maria twice!*

Next thing I knew, I was in a small Mexican town, and I needed to get married *on paper.* Maria and I signed the paper across the park. Maria came with some carne asada tacos. That was the first time that I'd ever eaten any tacos. After that, Maria drove off in another car.

The men I was with told me *I couldn't see Maria anymore until tomorrow when I married her.*

"Okay," I said.

One hombre in the car had a *real gun* and handed it over to me. Having had some margaritas, I joked around with them, waving around the gun in my hand, about how scary it was to get married, and accidentally, I shot the gun in the air! *Bang! I did not expect it to be loaded!* I had no idea! Embarrassed, I handed the gun back calmly and pretended that I did it on purpose. I grinned as wide as I could.

It was the morning of the wedding now. The suit I had got ruined somehow. I was getting married *today* at 2:00 p.m. What could I do?

"Harold, can I ask you a big favor?"

"It's your wedding day, Stuart. Ask me *anything*."

"Do you have a black suit I can borrow?" Well, after a few margaritas, I was asking myself, "Am I sure I want to do this?" As hard as I could think, all the signs *were positive!* All the *lights were green, meaning go!* I knew that God had sent Maria in answer to my prayers. I would never be lonely again.

We got married, and it was a magical and wonderful wedding and reception. Being drunk and busy, I forgot to invite my parents to the wedding, but I had told them I had been planning it. I phoned my house from Mexico. When I told my mom that I was *now married*, she was speechless! And so was my father—they were both in shock! My sister's husband had to take the phone, and I told him all about what I could remember about the wedding.

"I've got pictures," I said.

But the real reason I did not invite them was because I loved Maria and was a quarter of a century old now (twenty-five) and I *did not care if they approved of Maria or not!*

Did we live happily ever after? Well, yes, but not so fast.

Next, we went on a honeymoon in Mexico in the town of Mazatland. It was wonderful. I had a credit card and only ten dollars in my pocket, but the hotels accepted my Master card as payment. We stayed at a cheap hotel, but we went to a fancy hotel for dinner and atmosphere. That night, I found out *two* important things about Maria on our honeymoon:

1.   One margarita, and she was gone. *Maria was not a drinker of alcohol—good!*
2.   In bed, I knew *for sure* I was her first man.

I knew I'd be happy now because I found the right woman. Now, to get Maria home to New Jersey, that was the next problem!

Back at my truck mirror company, my company's vice president, Randy, gave me a pay raise so I could get a nice apartment to bring Maria home to. I found one in Perth Amboy near the New Jersey Turnpike. It was nice, but there was a *problem getting Maria to the USA.* So I wrote a letter to Senator Harry Jones. *He remembered me!* And he *pulled some strings,* and Maria was instantly approved to come into the USA. Thank you, Senator Jones!

I picked up Maria at the Newark Airport and drove to our new apartment. We were a happily married couple. *She was worth the wait!* We were so in love that the kitchen in our apartment caught fire once as we were too romantically involved to notice!

I brought Maria to meet my family, and they were skeptical at first. But after knowing Maria for about six months, we were invited over for dinner.

Stuart's parents by now also loved Maria. Pretending to be angry, his father took me aside and said, "Well, Stuart, you really did it this time!" Then he smiled and said, "You made the right choice for a wife. At least, Stuart, *you did one thing right! Maria is great! You chose wisely!*"

CHAPTER SIXTEEN

Functional Alcoholic in New Jersey

Newlyweds and happily married to an alcoholic, Maria soon realizes that I am not a rich man; so she went out to look for work. She found a job as a sewing machine operator at a Perth Amboy clothing company.

Soon, back at the Detroit Dinosaur Truck Mirror Company, Vice President Andy and two of his secretaries gave a surprise wedding shower for Maria and me with lots of nice wedding gifts. And Andy also offered a job for Maria to work in the truck mirror factory. Randy was a *great boss!* Soon, a baby shower for Maria.

Before I knew what happened, we had a wonderful daughter, Myra. Randy gave me a pay raise so I could buy my first house, and my parents helped us with the down payment. I had everything a man could dream of. But me, I was *never* satisfied. I wanted more.

I was a *daily drunk*, and I wanted *more* out of life! Then I dreamed that I could be like Randy. To everyone's surprise and mine, one day I just *quit my job!* Now I could drink alcohol and work for myself—great idea, so I thought.

My big idea was to start my *own advertising agency*, and I tried. It was called Action-Man Advertising. I had no training at all, except my observation of a real advertising agency that worked producing flyers and catalogs for the Detroit Dinosaur Truck Mirror Company. When drinking alcohol, I decided that I could do that *too*, even better, but I could not. Action-Man Advertising lasted only a couple of months.

I had a desk at home, thinking, *I am my own boss. I can keep liquor in my desk and drink all day long. Isn't it great having your own business?*

Action-Man Advertising business did *not succeed* in paying the bills. It failed. To top things off, I read in the newspaper that New Jersey Senator Harry Jones was sent to federal prison after an FBI sting about "taking bribes." Something they called "abscam." And winter was here.

I took a bottle of booze from my home office desk drawer and lifted it to my lips. I wondered, *Why can't I become a success like Randy? What's wrong with my life?* That night, I drank alcohol until I faded into oblivion.

While searching the classifieds for possible employment, I happened across an announcement for an Alcoholics Anonymous meeting in my New Jersey town. I "guessed" I *might* have a drinking problem, but I was too scared to check out that meeting. One snowy night, I got drunk to get enough courage to try to see what it was all about.

I sat outside a church parking lot in my car, drinking in the cold white night until the meeting was just about over. Then bravely, I walked in. The *only* word I heard spoken was *God!*

Oh, no! Religious nutcases! I thought to myself. No one at that meeting came to speak with me nor me to them. I was a scared "newcomer" who needed help and did not have a clue back then what twelve-step meetings were all about. I never went back to a twelve-step meeting until many, many years later, until out of desperation when I was nearly dead. Now my drinking life continued as I knew no other way to live. I had let the miracle of Alcoholics Anonymous pass right by me.

So how *would* a person of "superior intelligence," such as myself, get a *good* boss and a *good* job at the same time when nobody would hire him. *Start another business!*

Yes, it was *springtime now!* Most anybody *can paint a house*, I thought. *How hard could it be?* I saw some local painters down the road from my house and observed that they were in and out of a home, painting a *whole house* in only *one day!* They used an airless spray-painting system.

I walked over to the painting company owner. I asked, "Hi, I'm a neighbor and also a homeowner. Just curious, how much would a house like this cost to have your company paint it?"

He told me, "Four thousand dollars would cover labor and paint," and that his company catered to wealthy homeowners.

Wow! I thought. *Four thousand in one day! Easy booze money for sure!*

Next, I went into my local town to Louie's loan shark company and told him point-blank, "Louie, to be honest with you, I'm *flat broke* and *unemployed*. But I am a US Navy veteran, and I want *you* to *loan* me $1,000 so I can buy an airless spray-painting machine and some equipment. Louie, I've already been turned down by *all the banks*. Louie, you *are my last hope!*"

Louie the Loan Shark said, "Stuart, you just came to the right place. One minute...you *are a homeowner* too, right?"

"Yes," I said.

"Go to in the back room and talk to my partner, Ricky."

Ricky looked familiar. *Don't I know him?* Turned out Ricky was US Navy on duty in Scotland with me!

"Tell you what, Stuart," Ricky said, "you have a good idea. Out of the *goodness of my heart*, I will give you the money at 25 percent interest. But don't make me sorry I gave you the money, okay? Do we have a deal, Stuart?"

"Yes, we do," I said.

"You've *got the money!*"

"I won't let you down, Ricky. You have *my word!*" I told him.

I was driving a 1965 Mustang convertible, and I used my limited experience in advertising to make my own flyers and advertisements. I designed a homeowner's contract to benefit my desperate financial interests, which gave me some cash up front.

The homeowner would pay for the entire cost of the retail price of the paint in advance and 30 percent down of the estimated labor cost up front, and the balance would be due immediately upon completion of my paint job.

With the 30 percent down on my first contract, I bought an extension ladder and some paintbrushes, and more booze, and after that day, Painting Power-One-Day-House-Painting was born! My Mustang convertible had a twenty-eight-foot ladder tied on top.

I had no idea how to use the airless spray gun or how to properly prepare and paint a house. I ran a "help wanted" ad for *experienced painters.*

Soon, I had Jake, sixty years old but with over thirty-five years' experience, and a young kid. Now I was ready to start painting my first job, which was a very large two-story white house. Jake showed me how to use the airless spray gun, and I soon became good at it. I spray-painted the house body. Jake painted the trim, and the young kid handed us stuff and cleaned up. I charged $2,000 for the first house. *It looked good!* We were all happy!

Next day, the same lady called me up, all in a panic. She said, "*All the paint is peeling off the house by itself!*" The first house I painted turned into a nightmare because we had painted over oxidized white paint, which was like painting over a powdered *chalk surface.* The new paint we put on did not stick to the house surface.

Back at the Old Paint Store, the clerk told me about a paint additive that will make any paint *stick* to *anything* and also about another machine called a Power-Wash machine which hooked up to a garden hose and blasted high-pressure water to clean up a house fast.

After two more jobs, I paid Louie the Loan Shark his money in full and got *another loan* and bought the power-wash machine too. Now, I could charge homeowners for a power-wash also!

I had lost money on that first house because later, I gave the lady all her money back. But it was a good learning experience.

As more and more painting jobs came to me, my fear of climbing ladders increased. I was so afraid to start a new job that I had to have a few drinks of alcohol before I could do the job or even go to the location.

Yes, I was a "functioning alcoholic," all right. I'd show up and even work all day while drinking alcohol, mostly beers, all day long for me and my paint crew!

As a result, I took dangerous risks, like if the ladder was too short, I put it on a car roof and then climbed the ladder in fear of each step. Also, to paint with airless spray, I only held onto the ladder with one hand, and I'd push the ladder away from the building with my foot to paint the "ladder marks" behind the ladder. One day while doing this on an aluminum house, when I set the ladder back down on the wet paint, the ladder started to slide sideways like a knife across a buttered pan. The ladder was going down with me on it! Being drunk I had no fear.

Good thing I was drunk! I steered the ladder while it was going down, and the top landed in a hedge. I realized I was lucky I survived that fall on that day.

I discovered some homeowners paid well, while others did not pay at all. Some were difficult. Apartment owners sometimes were okay, but after one last dangerous drunken climb way up on a four-story apartment with a newly bought fifty-foot extension ladder, well, even while drunk, I was *scared half to death up there*! To top it off, when it was all done, the owner pointed to the top in the middle and said, "You missed a spot!"

I know that I did not, but sure enough, I saw a black mark in the middle of the fourth floor side. Fearfully, I slowly climbed all the way up the fifty-foot ladder *again! It was only a moth!* And it *flew away!* "Never again will I be on a high ladder," I vowed.

Winter was coming. Painting jobs were fewer and far between, and I was *tired* of painting! My money went to alcohol.

"But one-day house painting was a good idea," I said to myself. "I know, I'll make a franchise out of it, and soon, *Painting-Power One Day House Painting* will be a household word!" So I bought a home movie camera and made a pretty good documentary and sales plan and, even then, showed the franchise movie idea at a New Jersey Holiday Inn to the public.

I was so drunk then I could hardly function at all. Even this surefire "get rich quick" idea soon failed all because I was a functioning alcoholic who could *only function while drinking alcohol*, and not very well at that.

In New Jersey, it was freezing cold, and the entire road up the hill to my house turned to ice, covered with snow. This happened because a cold rain turned into snow by afternoon in New Jersey. The heating bill to warm our house was astronomical and took all my money.

My house painting business was over and was at a standstill in winter. I bought a new Ford Granada. It was gray. I got a welding job. The work was dirty and dangerous, so I went in drunk one day and told my boss what I thought of him and was fired. Driving home on the icy freeways covered with snow, I stepped on my brakes hard to avoid hitting another car. I was tailgating another car on the freeway because the falling snow was coming down so hard that I could not even see where the road was! On the snowy days, people drove with lights on, so I followed another car closely and let *them* figure out where the road was! Yes, I was "tailgating" him.

The car in front of me suddenly stopped. I could see brake lights get bright in front of me, so I stepped on my brakes hard to avoid hitting the car in front. My car skidded around fast and stopped, facing the *wrong* direction on the New Jersey freeway! Good thing I was drunk. That would have really scared me if I'd been sober!

Wait, I got it, I thought as I took another sip of wine. *It's New Jersey. That's the problem! I am sure if I move to California, my family and I will be happy! I can start new, and I heard California pays for college in that state! Free college for me! I'm going there.*

I did not know then what I know now that when I moved to another place and *I was the real problem*, that I'd be the *first one to get there*. Therefore, "doing a geographic" would not help the real problem I had of alcoholism.

My mother suddenly *passed away*, and I crawled into my bottle, drinking heavily. My father got moved to a nursing home. There was no reason anymore for us to stay in New Jersey.

I put my house up for *rent* because maybe I could have income from it in California. I found a real estate broker who handled it. I could always sell it later.

He told me, "Nobody will pay that much rent for *your place*."

I said, "Yes, they will. It's a cool location." I did not tell him that when I drove my car up to my house in the icy winter. I was lucky if I made it up the hill. Sometimes it was so icy, I'd get halfway up and get stuck in the snow, and I'd have to walk the rest of the way home. Nor did I tell him how going down was better because you can "slide" down easily. My car became like a giant sled!

Maria's family in Mexico had moved closer to the California border by now. So our destination was a border town near Tijuana, Mexico. I knew that my new car could make the trip.

Now Myra and Maria and I were all excited and planned to see all the tourist sites we could along our trip by car from New Jersey to California. And yes, of course, Disneyland was on the list as well.

California, here we come!

Stuart's going to California would not solve his drinking problem because in twelve-step programs, this was called "doing a geographic." Stuart's alcohol problem would only get worse and stronger...

CHAPTER SEVENTEEN

Going Down in California

Crossing the United States from New Jersey, my family and I were excited we were leaving snowy New Jersey, heading for sunny California, and we made tourist stops along the way at the Grand Canyon and Petrified Forest. We walked around and took photos. And of course, we did Disneyland.

Then, we were headed to the border town near Mexico called San Ysidro, California. Maria's family had relocated to Tijuana, and Maria's brother owned a business in downtown Tijuana. So not knowing where to live at first, my family stayed in Tijuana with Maria's relatives right in the *center* of the downtown area near tourist spots on Revolution Avenue.

And I needed a drink, and soon I found myself "checking out" the nightclubs and bars in Tijuana. And soon, "topless" bars became places to hang out and to drink tequila and beer and to watch the dancers dance into the nighttime hours while Maria visited with her relatives and spoke to them in Spanish. I felt "left out" of it.

I soon moved my family to the border town of San Ysidro into a motel. I was still "unskilled" and a fish out of water in Mexico and California, but it was true that a California resident went to college cheaply. I soon enrolled at a local junior college to learn how to become a computer operator. Before too long, I managed to land a *midnight-shift* job in a hospital in downtown San Diego as a computer operator.

It was a job consisting of mounting rolls of computer tape and backing up hospital data. I was *reliable*. I never drank booze on the job, but every chance I got, I'd go to Mexico with Maria. She would stay and visit and talk Spanish with her family, and I would spend the evenings wandering the bars, drinking alcohol all night, and staring at boobs. But every time the ladies asked me to go to a room with them, I said no.

And that was the farthest I intended to go— *just looking*. After all, I had a good wife and just liked "looking." The bar girls knew this, and over time, some of the girls knew me well. It was a way to spend an evening. But inevitably, I got *drunk*. But then, before I knew it, I blacked out and came to. The more alcohol I drank, the more times I blacked out. When I woke up, I even found myself on stage *in front of strangers*! How *humiliating! Drunk out of my mind!*

Besides a poisoned headache hangover, when I got home, I was ashamed of my drunken behavior. *I never ever wanted or intended to be untrue to my truelove of my life in any way.* Alcohol was unpredictable. I could not stop drinking it.

Sometimes, only one beer would get me drunk, and at other times, I could drink all night with little effect. And I never knew for sure *what would happen* or *what stupid things I would end up doing* after I put alcohol in my brain! I'd go into blackouts and could not remember what I did the night before. My inhibitions were gone, and my judgment was impaired whenever I drank too much. I got real crazy like a zombie.

And sober, I'd never do anything but look at those girls and that would be enough, but after drinking, I'd want to check them out closer. I guess *that was the very reason that they would always give me the first beer free,* knowing that for me, after one, I would want more!

It was to me back then an unexplainable baffling mystery, wondering why I could not be like other people. My family was *still living in a crummy motel for crying out loud—more days flew by drunken and oblivion.*

While lifting the alcohol to my lips, I thought, *I'm too fat! Maybe if I go juice fasting and get in shape…it's my health! I know I can just decide*

185

not to drink alcohol anymore. That should be easy.

I began juice fasting for the next twenty-one days and made up my mind to start jogging. My wife, Maria, and my daughter, Myra, would go to the San Diego zoo and to free concerts at the wild animal park every Sunday, and we would go to San Diego County parks so they all could *ride bikes* and I could jog along while they rode bikes. Maria rode a bike too! It was fun. We did this on weekends. On weekdays, I would run in a field across from the motel near the Mexican border fence, and my daughter would ride her bike while I jogged. Things were good then because while on the juice fast, I had not had a drink in *two weeks!* I was finally sober for first time in years.

On this afternoon, it was almost sunset. I was running in the field across the Mexican border. My daughter, Myra, was following me on her new bike. We passed a large water pipe tunnel sticking out the side of a small hillside alongside the USA-Mexico border fence, and inside were *people* who looked afraid to come out of that pipe.

Stuart suddenly realized these people were crossing the border from Tijuana to the United States illegally, and border patrol police seemed to be everywhere.

Stuart was wearing his bright red jogging suit, and his daughter Myra was wearing a blue jogging suit also following him, riding the jogging path on her bike.

"I don't believe these people are any danger to us, Myra. Let's ride around the trail again to take another look at that pipe."

"Okay," said Myra.

We rode around past the pipe, and to our amazement, 287 new joggers came out of that pipe in perfect running in pairs formation, following us to the main road and disappeared into this town.

These were happy memories because I did *not* drink then. So after twenty-one days of being sober on the juice fast, I was starving for real food. I obsessed over food. The juice fast had worked.

I lost twenty pounds. On the twenty-first day, I found myself back in downtown Tijuana. I had not gone to any bars at all. My goal of the juice fast was thirty days. I passed a restaurant and could smell delicious, good Mexican food cooking.

Stuart's alcohol dependency returned unexpectedly. Then a stink in my thinking. *Maybe if I took just "one" drink of beer, it would "help me" forget about food!*

So before I knew it, I drank about five beers in a row and was in an alcoholic *trance* and back in that restaurant eating like a pig! I relapsed; alcohol grabbed me *again*.

After eating, I felt good and relieved, and the hunger was all gone. But the *craving to have another drink strongly persisted*! It was also then when I first realized that I had been *drinking against my own free will*! I did not *want* to drink; *I had to*! The insatiable obsession for alcohol was back. Stuart suddenly began to realize he could not stop drinking that he was "hooked" on alcohol.

When I got home, I explained what happened to Maria that I broke my juice fast. She told me that I did good for the twenty-one days and that she was *proud of me*! I was starting to act like a new and better man, she said. Little did she know.

But it was not really a "health-food" problem. I was an alcoholic, and I did not even know what that meant back then. So things continued to get *worse*—heavy drinking even when I did not want to drink. *I could not stop!* I *had* to have alcohol now *several times a day*!

Not on the juice fast anymore and drinking again, I still tried to rationalize that it was not the alcohol at all, thinking alcohol was my best friend and continued jogging. In the border town, a couple of blocks down from the border field that I always had jogged in, was an "American" *topless girl* place that had just opened up for business. I guess I could go in for one drink.

One afternoon after I ran the field across from my motel while my daughter followed me as usual on her bike and just before we were supposed to go back home, I told her, "Hey, I just want to check something out in that new place." She followed me to the topless bar entrance. "I'll just be a second, Myra. I'll be right out."

I went in and had a beer, thinking one beer wouldn't hurt, and to my horror, I forgot all about my daughter waiting outside for me on her bike!

Finally, a dancer told me, "Hey mister! Is that *your daughter out there*? What's the matter with you anyway?"

Pitiful and incomprehensible demoralization! *What had I done?* I blacked out and forgot all about my darling daughter! *How could I have done that? My drinking was getting bad!* I thought to myself.

That was my first wake-up call. Maybe if I moved to a *better area away* from Tijuana, I could "control" my drinking. To top this idea off, one night, I was driving home drunk. I thought I was sober enough to drive home and I could handle a "few" drinks. It was a dark night and raining. Suddenly, I saw my headlights shine in the dark rain onto people's faces. I *slammed* on my brakes! The people wore *dark clothes.* I could not see them at all; they blended in. If they had not turned to look at my car, I would have run them over! And once again, another wake-up call! I swore off drinking and driving that night—again. But Stuart's dependency on alcohol continued to get worse. He was slowly crossing the invisible line to becoming a daily drinker.

My midnight-shift computer jobs helped pay the bills. I showed up as a functioning alcoholic, and after a couple of years, I got a better computer job in downtown Los Angeles. The new job *paid well*, and now I could afford to buy a "new" house. Maria and my daughter and I were all excited! First, we moved to an apartment while *our* new house was being built *just for us! How exciting!*

I wanted a good home for my family, and I got one. What more could a man want? I have it *all* now—a happy home and a *good* family in a brand-new house.

But I was still not happy. I wanted *more*, and I was a functioning alcoholic. As long as I drank every day, I could function.

Happy in our new home, my daughter had her *own room*. My wife and I had a master bedroom. We had a huge backyard and a three-car garage. I had my new car, and also now I could buy a pickup truck.

My midnight-shift computer job took up most of my time. Even though I didn't need to be there until 11:00 p.m., I liked to get there at 10:30 p.m. at least. I worked in downtown Los

Angeles at a five-story building which was a factory that manufactured "furniture." All night long, I was the *only one* in the factory, and I was a full-time computer operator. I ran computer programs to back up the factory's financial data on *reels* of computer tape.

I was a reliable and dependable employee. *I didn't drink on the job!*

In the morning, the drive back home took *two to four hours!* So after a while, it seemed I never had *any time at home*. Maria also worked in an office now. I was always at work or driving to work. There was no time except weekends to be home. Soon, I came up with the idea of putting a camper shell on the back of my pickup truck. After months of working a midnight shift in downtown Los Angeles, I'd be *very tired*, and I'd park my pickup truck at some restaurant along the way going back home and *sleep* a few hours before returning to the remaining journey home—to my very *nice home*. Besides, after a nap, I felt better to drive home "awake."

Stuart's alcohol addiction slowly crossed over from his being a daily drinker to an all-day drinker.

Gradually, I became extremely efficient at my midnight job, and while the computer program would run on its own for hours on end at midnight, I'd go out for lunch breaks at 2:00 a.m.

I had time to cruise Skid Row and Hollywood in my pickup truck (with a *bed in the back*)!

The insanity that came with me drinking was about to strike again. Even though I never drank on the job, I thought, *A lunch hour drink is okay!* I'd have about *one* hour before I had to get back to work. I drank a bottle of wine, which I kept in the back of my truck. My pickup truck had back seat access through the back window in the cab.

On this night at 2:00 a.m. in Hollywood, there were some "interesting" looking ladies walking up and down the street. Lots of them! *Both* in *Skid Row* and in *Hollywood. Dang! I have to get back to work*, I thought.

It was a Friday night, or should I say Saturday morning between 2:00 a.m. and 3:00 a.m. I had just got paid, and from the ready teller, I had $200 cash in my wallet intended for the next weekend with *my family*! But now, I saw all these ladies of the evening all over the place. The alcohol I drank started to relax me. These ladies were very tempting to "check out." But I needed to get back to work. I turned the car around to head back to work. *Where the hell am I now? I'm in Hollywood!*

Suddenly, a *very pretty face* was in my window close up while I was at a stoplight at Hollywood and Vine.

"Hey, mister! Help me! *I need to get out of here!*"

I'd been drinking, so my mind was hazy now. Out of kindness and concern, *without thinking*, I unlocked the door and let her in! And a *perfect* stranger sat next to me. My drunken eyes said she looked *like a princess*—all dressed up in a *fancy gown*.

"Where do you want to go?" I asked. "You know, lady, you look just like a *princess*!"

She said to me, "Thanks, *I am a princess*! Anywhere you're going is fine with me!"

"Well then, princess, I have to go back to work!" I replied. "I'm on my lunch hour! *I'm sorry! I can't* help you, lady."

She said, "*Pull over a minute*. It won't take long. *You won't be late!* I promise! I'm Brenda. I'm an actress. And you *are* in *Hollywood*, you know! And your name is?"

"Oh! Oh, it's...er...ah...Stuart!" I stammered.

I parked the car on the side of a dark building on an empty street. Then, Brenda unbuttoned her blouse and showed me.

"This is how I *audition* for movies!" she explained. "Do you like what you see, Stuart?"

"Of course, I do, Brenda, but *really*, I *must* go! I'm on my lunch break. That was a nice show, Brenda. Now, *how much do I owe you?*"

"*Nothing*, Stuart! I don't need your money. I'm an actress! Now, go to work, Mr. Stuart, but come back for me. And I'll let you take me out of this town! I think God wants me to be with *you*, Stuart! I don't know why!"

Brenda got out of my truck and shut the door hard. I went back to work and wondered, *What just happened? Was I dreaming! That was crazy! Will I ever see Brenda again? Should I see her? Does or did she really need my help?*

I was back at my midnight-shift job and completely *confused* from that meeting with Brenda. Then, I realized *my wallet was gone!* That lady stole my wallet!

I got my reports ready. It was 6:00 a.m. now. I'm out of work, and I drive back to where Brenda was. *Daytime* looks different in Hollywood than nighttime. No resemblance. No sign of Brenda or my wallet at all!

All day long, Stuart's alcohol dependency got him threw out of his own home! He had become a homeless drunk.

So I took the long ride back home. That weekend, at home, I was drinking heavily, becoming a crazy madman. I started smashing things and yelling in a blackout *rage*! And Maria told me to *get out of the house and stay out* and that I probably could not find another woman other than her to *put up with my drinking*!

During the next couple of weeks, I began to learn to sleep in the truck bed of my pickup truck with a camper shell on it. It was like a little house in there. I started sleeping in the camper truck on weekdays in the local *county park*. Very nice there! Very quiet! A *homeless* lady showed me where I could get free food. There was a list of free food places posted on a church window. I went back home now only on weekends.

Maria was a good wife, and I loved her. She washed my clothes for work. When I was *not drinking*, I was a nice guy, but *I couldn't stop*!

I got drunk on that bottle of scotch *that night*. I got pulled over for *drunk driving*!

Two highway patrol officers, a man and a woman, *beat me* with their "dream stick" to teach me a lesson. I woke up in jail in the drunk tank next morning with a bunch of other drunks!

"I'm sorry, Maria," I told her. "I will *never leave you! I promise you that. I love you!*

So now, I was still working my midnight-shift job. Traffic was bad to and from work as usual.

I was drunk all of the time when not working in Los Angeles or stuck in traffic to and from there. Again, I was bored. There must be more to life than this. I went to court for drunk driving but hired a lawyer to reduce the charge to "reckless wet..." whatever that was and again missed a chance to get sober.

Drunk driver Stuart missed his chance to get sober by having a slick lawyer get him "off the hook." So Stuart continued his alcohol dependency, and it got worse.

CHAPTER EIGHTEEN

The Pavement Princess

Back at my night-shift job in downtown Los Angeles, the factory had "security" cameras mounted outside, so I could see who was outside at the front door and rear entrances. My factory was located only about ten city blocks from Skid Row. It was a five-story building. And I was usually the *only person* in the *whole factory* at night, *especially on Friday nights!*

This night, someone was *banging* on the rear entrance door! I pushed the speaker button. "Who is it?" I asked.

"It's Brenda, *your pavement princess!* Remember me, Stuart? You gave me a ride once?"

"Yes, Brenda," I answered. "It was nice! How could I forget?"

"I *found* your wallet, Stuart. I want to *give it back to you!* And well, Stuart, I do need *your* help again!"

I saw her in the security camera. She looked alone. "Can we talk? Can I come in?"

I buzzed her in, unlocking the door.

"My camera crew will wait outside," she added.

"Camera crew?" I asked. "What the heck are you talking about, Brenda?"

"Stuart, it will only take a couple of hours, and *nobody will know we were ever here*! Can my crew at least come in to look around?"

"No, Brenda!" I answered. "It's *not my company*!"

She handed me a bottle of peach brandy. I took a drink of it.

"*Relax, Stuart!*" she said as she took off her shirt. "*Please?*"

When I saw her that way, she *knew she had power over me*. I was speechless!

"Tell them to come on in, Stuart," she urged.

"Okay," I said.

"Hey, what's this room?" a male voice said.

"No, you can't go into *that* room because it's the company president's boardroom!" I shouted.

"It's perfect! We'll shoot the movie in here!"

"Shoot a movie!" I exclaimed. "What kind of movie?"

"Stuart, I'm an *amateur* adult movie star, Stuart. I sell my movies to local adult stores— *instant money!*

"Who else will be in the movie with you?" I asked.

"Just my girlfriend Marsha here and one other person..."

"Who is that?" I asked in bewilderment.

"*You, Stuart! You* will be in my movie! And what's more, *I'll pay you $1,000!*"

"Listen, Brenda, I do like you...how could I not? How did you find me?"

"Your wallet had your business card in it, which said, 'Stuart McPherson: Senior Computer Operator, Big Empire Furniture Manufacturing Company.' Last time, in case I needed to find you again, I took your wallet!"

"So why do you need me again, Brenda? What could I possibly do for you?" I asked her. "I'm working here all night alone."

Brenda said, "Stuart, I *told* you I was a movie star, didn't I?"

"Well, you did, Brenda, but I thought you were *only kidding!*"

"Honey, this is Hollywood. We *don't kid about that!*"

"Okay, then how can I help?" I said to her.

"I *have a movie contract*, and I want to return your $200 back to you too. And I need to *make a movie tonight!* So if you help me, I'll pay you $1,000 cash. Tonight my film crew wants to film inside *your company, right now!* We need a shoot location!"

Then, she showed me the cash: ten new crisp one-hundred-dollar bills! Brenda said,

"Here is the thousand-dollar cash in advance in your wallet, Stuart!"

I said, "Okay, I'll do it!"

Last thing I vaguely remembered was that I was *drunk* again and someone was filming it all and also taking *flash* photos.

It was on a *Friday* night. Most of that night was an *alcoholic blur to me*! Early Saturday morning, no one was supposed to come into the factory. It was closed on weekends. I woke up just in time. The outside security cameras I monitored showed the company's president's car *coming*! Occasionally, and only *sometimes*, he did come in to work in his office on Saturday mornings.

"Brenda!" I shouted. "You've got to hide! You and your crew need to get out of here! *The boss is coming!*

The boss comes in. "Hi, Mr. President, good morning, sir," I said.

"You're *still here*, Stuart?"

"Yes, sir!" I answered respectfully. "Just making sure the reports are correct before I leave, sir!"

Now, if the president had opened his conference room door, I'd have been fired! Luckily, he just got something out his office and left.

On his way out, the president turned to me and said, "You're doing a mighty fine job here, Stuart! This company needs more reliable, dependable employees *like you*!"

"Thanks, boss!" I answered. "I *love* this company!

Brenda and her "movie crew" had already gone a minute later and disappeared into the morning LA fog. The conference room looked fine. But as I grabbed the keys to my car to leave, I suddenly noticed something funny— something just wasn't quite right. *My wallet was gone! Again!* Not only with the thousand dollars in it, but *fifty* more of my own money that I had that night on me. *Brenda had tricked me again!*

Instead of driving home to my town which was a two-hour drive, this Saturday morning I was in no hurry. I knew I was still *not* on good terms with my wife. I was going to take her out to dinner tonight with that fifty dollars. Luckily, I had stashed thirty dollars in cash in my pickup truck glove compartment.

I decided to leave my vehicle at the factory parking lot and go for a walk in downtown Los Angeles to a nearby eating food court to get a cup of coffee and a *good* breakfast before my long two-hour drive back home.

Lots of people around this restaurant were homeless. Some tried to panhandle me. This was normal here as it was *next* to the Skid Row area. But inside the restaurant, I felt safe, and after eating breakfast and drinking several cups of coffee, the effects of last night's drinking were almost completely gone.

As I was getting ready to pay my breakfast bill and go back to get my truck and go home, I suddenly saw someone else eating breakfast across the restaurant. *Hey!* I thought. *That looks like Marsha! That is Marsha…from last night!*

Marsha was alone, just sitting there, staring into space with a coffee cup in front of her.

"Hi, Marsha. Mind if I join you?"

Marsha looked *shocked* to see me!

"I had nothing to do with it! It was Brenda's idea!" she said.

"Hey, I'm not here to fight with *you* or anyone else, Marsha. Actually, I've got a headache, and I don't remember anything of what happened last night. I just wish someone like you—Marsha, isn't it?—can tell me just what's going on around here because I haven't got a clue!

Marsha sat with her cup of coffee. "Well, can you buy me some breakfast *if* I tell you?"

"Anything you want, Marsha!" I replied.

Marsha ordered an extra superlarge breakfast and ate it all like she had not eaten for weeks. I could hardly believe it! The plate of food was gone in minutes.

"Oh, Stuart, *thanks!* I feel much better now!" she said.

"So what's *really* going on around here, Marsha?" I asked. "Just *who* is Brenda, anyway?"

Marsha said, "Listen, Stuart...I love Brenda, so please don't tell her it was me that tells you these things, okay?"

"Okay, I won't," I promised.

"First of all...Brenda *is not an actress. She does not live in Hollywood*, but it is true that she makes and sells her photographs and movies to adult stores. And *she does go to auditions!*"

"Hey, that shouldn't be such a big deal in Hollywood," I said.

"No, Stuart, that is still *not* the *real* reason. She is also in her thirties."

"She don't look like it," I said. "And *that* should not be a problem either in Hollywood. So what *else* is going on, Marsha? Tell me. Must be something else?"

"No, Stuart, I *can't tell you* Brenda's 'big secret.'"

"Well, Marsha, okay then...at least tell me what happened last night."

"Stuart, after you drank the whole pint bottle of peach brandy, our movie cameraman and Brenda's photographer started shooting *the movie*. Then *you* slobbering drunk went crazy, Stuart, and started telling me and Brenda about how in your Navy days you had some fun Scottish girls. Because she said you told her you were very good at pleasing women in bed, even better than most other women can please each other."

"Marsha, I don't remember *any* of *that*. What happened to my wallet? *Why* did she take it?"

"She don't want your wallet. Stuart, I told you. It's a *secret*. But I can tell you this. *The money was not hers to give you!* That $1,000 was for *someone else*. Brenda does not look like it, but *she is very sick and needs $1,000 every day for her medicine!* It's *not her fault*, Stuart, so don't get mad at her!"

"Sick?" I asked. "*She is sick?*"

"She is home, trying to *get well* right now."

Now I was really confused. Should I feel sorry for her and forgive her?

"Listen, Marsha...I *really* need a drink. You really got me confused. You've got me worried about Brenda instead of me being angry with her," I confessed. "One more thing, Marsha... when you see Brenda, tell her that I care about her and ask her if there is anything I can do to help her."

"Stuart," she answered, "why don't *you* go tell her yourself! But *keep me out of it*! And don't tell her how you found her. Promise?"

"Yes, I promise, Marsha," I said. "Please tell me where she is!"

"Stuart, you *won't* need your car. She lives only a few blocks from here. She lives in *Skid Row!* Go down three blocks, turn left, then four more, and turn right. She is in the third cardboard box on the left!"

This was just too crazy! My truck was safe back in the company parking lot. It was about 11:00 a.m. now on a Saturday morning in downtown Los Angeles. I had just eaten a good breakfast, and *I* felt good. But before I tried to find out if Brenda *really did live in Skid Row* and not in Hollywood, I did *need* a drink! So I bought the same thing again that Brenda had brought me the night before—peach brandy. I drank *half the bottle*. I put my necktie in my pocket. I tried to look like a homeless person, and I seemed to blend into Skid Row, walking along the street with a pint of brandy in my hand.

Okay, three blocks down, turn left. This looked like Skid Row, all right—*all these people* sleeping on the sidewalk. cardboard boxes, tarps, shopping carts, *lots* of cardboard condos. *Unbelievable!* People were dressed in rags. The entire three blocks were lined with homeless people living there. *Four more blocks and turn right.* This couldn't be true. Brenda could *never* live around here! *Turn right. The third cardboard box on the left.* Sure enough, there was a very *neat* large cardboard box there. Did I *dare* check to see if Brenda was *really* inside? Not yet. First, a *large gulp* of peach brandy. Okay, *now* I was ready.

"Hey, Brenda! Are you inside there? It's me, Stuart! Don't worry. I'm *not mad at you.* I just want to help you!"

Just then, a flap in the cardboard box opened up, and Brenda's tired, pretty face appeared.

"Stuart?" she said in a squeaky voice. "I'm sleeping. Can you come back later?"

"Not really," I said. "I have to go back to my hometown. I would like to talk with you. Can I get you some breakfast before I leave town?"

"Okay. Just give me a *few minutes* to get ready, and I'll come with you."

So I was waiting fifteen minutes outside this cardboard box, hoping nobody would recognize me. It was broad daylight.

"Listen, Brenda, it's okay. Maybe next week. I've really got to get going."

"No, Stuart, wait, *please*! I'll only be a minute!"

I took a sneak peek into the side flap of the carboard box and saw Brenda with a large hypodermic needle in her hand. She was "tying" off her arm. I could see in the sunbeam shining on her arm that her arm was *black and blue*! She was looking for a vein to stick the needle in. Brenda had watery black stuff in a spoon, which she heated up with a cigarette lighter. She seemed oblivious that I was watching her through the cardboard flap. She loaded the needle with black liquid and stuck it in her arm.

Then, it dawned on me what Brenda's "secret" was. Brenda was a *heroin addict!*

"Okay, Stuart, I feel better now. Let's go!" she said. "Where is your truck?"

"I walked here, Brenda. Where would you like to go for breakfast?"

Brenda said, "Stuart, there is nothing in this town for me. If you really want to help me, take me to *your town with you*."

"Are you sure, Brenda? I *don't* have *anywhere* you can stay."

"I can live in the back of *your* pickup truck. It's sure a lot better than a cardboard box!"

"You have a valid point there. But I don't even know you, Brenda."

"*Just* until I find a place of my own, Stuart. *I won't be a bother. I promise!*"

"I'm not sure *that's* a good idea," I reasoned. "But I'll take you anyway!"

"I'm going to pack my things up," she then said. "Come inside, Stuart."

I went inside her cardboard box. I was in a cardboard box on Skid Row with a homeless heroin addict with her. *How low could I go?*

I was supposed to be taking my wife out to dinner tonight. I must be crazy! Now I was driving my long two-hour ride, which now seemed like an *endless* ride, with a *lady* inside my camper. And my pager was going off!

My wife was calling me on my pager. I was very late. I knew she was worried. As I lifted the rest of the whiskey to my lips, I was asking, "How do I ever get myself into these predicaments?"

I stopped at a pay phone and phoned my lovely, devoted wife. Brenda was peacefully sleeping like a log in the camper truck bed on the mattress inside.

"Maria, sorry I'm late. I had a flat tire and ran out of gas too!" I lied. "Don't worry, my love. I'm on my way home *now*. I'll be home soon."

Lucky for me that during the week, I was *also* "homeless" and stayed days sleeping in the pickup truck in the county park. I had other homeless "friends" there, and my county park homeless friends were sitting at a picnic table, waiting for the 3:00 p.m. free food truck to arrive. I *knew* them all.

"Wake up, Brenda!" I said. "These people are good friends of mine. They will take care of you."

"You sure, Stuart?"

"Yes, Brenda. I've lived in this park for a while now. These are good people. They will show you where free food and clothes are. Don't worry, Brenda. I'll be back to check up on you next Monday."

"Hey, Stuart!" she said. "I can take care of myself. I like it here already. *Thank you, Stuart!*"

And I drove off and went home to spend the rest of the weekend with my lovely family. Little did I know that soon, I'd *really* be homeless too.

Finally, I was late getting home, but I was home. My wife, Maria, and my daughter were waiting for me.

"What took you so long, Stuart? Have you been drinking again?"

"Yes, I have, Maria," I admitted honestly.

"Why, Stuart? *Why?*"

"I don't know why!" I explained. "I always drink again when I don't know what will happen. I'm sorry. Listen, I don't want to fight, Maria. I worked all night, and I'm tired! I screwed up again. Let me take a nap!"

So I went up to my home bedroom and slept. When I awoke, I saw the angry, hurt faces of Maria and my daughter.

"Stuart, we were cleaning and washing up your pickup truck for you as a surprise for you, and we found a small lady's suitcase in the camper. Who does it belong to, Stuart?"

I just looked at them, not knowing what to say.

"Don't lie to us! Who *is* she?"

"She? What do you mean? I don't know what you're talking about!"

"Recognize *these photos,* Stuart?"

Oh my god! Maria had in her hands X-rated *photos* of Brenda and me from *last Saturday night!*

"We found *these* in the suitcase! Now *get out of this house! Now,* Stuart, and *don't come back...ever!*"

It was Sunday morning. I was leaving my wife's house. My daughter and wife were trying to *smash* my pickup truck with *sticks*! I drove away.

What are the neighbors going to think? I was thinking as I drove away to an unsure fate.

Stuart's alcohol-impaired judgment and his poor choices was summed up in the acronym PAID: Pitiful and Incomprehensible Demoralization.

CHAPTER NINETEEN

The Road Dog

So all day on Sunday, I was sleeping at my usual place in the county park. *I really was homeless now!* Good thing I would start work Monday night again. I missed my wife, Maria, but I didn't blame her. It was my fault. I had become a liar, a cheat, and a thief.

Well, I guess I could try to find Brenda. I asked my homeless friends, "Hey, what happened to my friend Brenda?"

"She's okay," they told me. "She left with a senior citizen, an *eighty-year-old guy* named Roscoe. Roscoe comes here all the time looking for dates and checking out ladies in the park. He has a paycheck coming in every month since retired. He's a nice old guy with a pension. Your friend Brenda will be okay. We told you we'd *look out* for her."

"Thanks," I answered.

"Also, we told her if she wants to work, try *Main Street*."

"Work?" I asked.

"That's where all the *other* girls hang out."

"Thanks," I said. "Tell her I'm looking for her if you see her again."

"Okay, sure, Stuart, we will!"

I went to drive up and down Main Street to get to know more about it. There were mostly motels and fast-food restaurants on that street. Then, I went back to the park and slept until midnight. At midnight Sunday, I was wide awake because, as you know, I worked the midnight shift in downtown Los Angeles—Monday night to Friday night. I was not at home with my wife tonight because I got thrown out.

I was *very lonely*. I guess that was *one* of the reasons I was looking at those ladies that night in Los Angeles. I didn't want to be alone. I needed a lady's companionship. I needed my wife.

But for now, I cruised up and down Main Street, getting to know what was there. I did notice two ladies walking in the dark. And only one fast food place was open.

I went in there to eat a burger and fries and got some coffee. After being tossed out of my home and being homeless, I was not ready to drink again—*yet*.

It was nighttime, early evening, in the fast-food place. I saw a few scattered people sitting around the tables. And I saw a very *pretty* lady wearing a T-shirt, and she was wearing new blue jeans. I looked *closer*. She looked familiar.

Do I know her? It couldn't be! She looked *different—all cleaned up* with a *different hairstyle.*

"Is that *you*, Brenda?

The lady got up and said, "Hi, Stuart!"

It was Brenda, all cleaned up. "Stuart, this is Roscoe, my *new friend!* He took care of me today and bought me some clothes and paid a whole week's rent for me in the Anytime Motel!"

"Hi, Mr. Roscoe, nice to meet you!" I said. "Thanks for taking such good care of her."

Brenda said to me, "I told Roscoe *all* about you that *you* are my *road dog* who looks out for me."

Roscoe politely said, "Nice to meet *you*, Mr. Stuart. *Please* let me *see* Brenda at least once a week," Roscoe added.

What's a "road dog"? I was thinking.

"Yes, *I am* Brenda's *road dog* and proud of it!" I answered spontaneously. "Mr. Roscoe, just be good to her and things will be fine. Treat her right! And...*Brenda* calls the shots, *not me!* I just like to make sure she is okay. So don't worry about me, Roscoe. Just treat her *nice!* Am I understood?"

Brenda said to Roscoe, "Listen, honey, I need to speak to my road dog alone. Can you go home to *your wife* now, Roscoe, and come back tomorrow?"

Roscoe politely left and drove away in his brand-new Oldsmobile. Brenda got into my pickup truck cab. We drove down Main Street. Brenda said, "Come with me, Stuart...I'll show you *my room*."

I told Brenda, "*I'm homeless now too*...my wife tossed me out!"

"You are *good*, Stuart. *I should pay you!* Then, she showed me her two *tattoos*—names of two ladies that were her "wives" at one time.

"*You* had a wife?" I asked her in amazement!

"Yes," Brenda said, "while I was in a woman's prison. *Two tattoos, two ladies' names*—they both died from heroin *overdoses*. Roscoe showed me where I could find connections here in this town and said he could find me a new girlfriend."

She told me, "I'm all ready to work. *You have to leave now.* You go sleep in your truck in the park. I have to go to work and walk the pavement of Main Street and see how many customers I can get before morning. But, Stuart, I want you to *pick me up* at 9:00 a.m."

I returned in the dark night to sleep in the park, and on Monday at 9:00 a.m., I picked up Brenda at her motel room.

"Where are we goin', Brenda?" I asked.

"To the connection," she said.

"What do you mean?" I asked, not understanding what she was talking about.

"I need to buy some more *black tar*," she explained.

"Black tar?" I asked. "What the heck is that?"

"Don't play dumb with me, Stuart," she said chastisingly. "I think you have figured out by now that I'm a *junkie*! Black tar is *heroin*. Don't you know anything? You are not *stupid*!"

"Neither are you, Brenda," I reassured her gently. "Brenda, I need a drink!"

"I've already bought some peach brandy for you," she replied. "And, Stuart, *I know you are an alcoholic, and you need your fix too! We make a good couple—an alcoholic and a heroin addict. Don't we?* Drink up, Stuart! Now, drive me to *this* address."

Brenda went up to a big house in Mountain Grove Estates with a very tall hedge in front. I parked in front of the hedge on the street.

Brenda said, "I'll be back in *ten* minutes, so wait for me. And no matter what happens, *don't leave!*"

Fifteen minutes went by, and no Brenda! I was sitting in front of this exclusive mansion in my camper/pickup truck. A police car drove by, then another, then five police cars surrounded the house. Cops got out of each squad car, running with guns drawn toward the house. I was dressed up in a shirt and tie because later on this Monday afternoon, I was going to Los Angeles, back to work on the midnight shift tonight like every other week.

So I asked the cop, "What's going on, officer?"

"It's a *drug raid!*" he announced. "We've been *monitoring* this house for the past six months, and today we are arresting everyone and shutting it down."

Then I told him, "Good job! You police are doing a great job protecting us citizens!"

So the police hauled people out the large house one by one in handcuffs and took them away. I was leaning on the side of my camper/pickup truck, wondering, *Where is Brenda? It's been over an hour now. I did not see the police take her. Where is she?*

Then, in front of me *in* the very large dark-green hedge, I noticed the leaves *were moving!* Brenda was hiding on top of the *big hedge!* She jumped out calmly as if *nothing* had happened. She had a big paper bag with her. Brenda said, "I'm okay, Stuart. I didn't get to go inside. I saw the cops, but the people inside threw away this bag near where I was hiding. *So it's mine now!*"

Inside the bag was a large supply of black tar, needles, and cash!

"Brenda, I've got to get out of here! I am feeling drunk now because after the cops left, I drank more peach brandy. And Brenda, I'm beginning to care about you *too much*. Now, you got me thinking of *you all the time!* I wish you'd stop working and stay in an apartment."

Brenda turned to me and said, "I'm lonely too. And you *can't stop drinking*, Stuart. I *can't stop using...it's who we are, Stuart! Accept it!* Stuart, but you are married."

"Where shall we go now?" I asked Brenda.

"Take me back to the motel. I have enough of everything I need to last me a while. Don't get me wrong...Stuart, I need my space."

All week long until next Friday night, I just went to my Los Angeles job at night and slept in the county park during the days and ate free lunches with the homeless people.

It was my last week night to work this week. It was Friday night again, and on Saturday morning, I will try to check up on my Pavement Princess. One important thing about me working Friday nights was when I got my paycheck. I worked hard, and I was a reliable employee all week so I could get paid a good salary to support Maria and my family. Maria was also working. It took both of us to pay the bills for my family.

But now, since I was out of my home and Maria did not want me around, I spent the money instead. My paycheck went to alcohol and seeing Brenda. And Brenda was expecting me because she knew I would have money on weekends.

I had not seen Brenda all week, which was unusual because she usually met me at the free lunch homeless places at noon. This week at the homeless noon lunch, I became friends with another street lady named Natasha.

At lunch last Wednesday, a pretty blond lady waved at me. "Hi, Stuart," she said.

I said, "Hi!"

She brought her food tray over to my lunch table.

"Hi, Stuart, I'm a *friend* of Brenda, a coworker, you might say. My name is Natasha. I'm Russian."

"Nice to meet you," I answered politely, admiring her Russian accent.

"Listen, Stuart," she continued, "you are Brenda's road dog, aren't you?"

"Yes, I am," I answered enthusiastically.

"You'll find out soon enough, so I might as well tell you..." Natasha said.

"Tell me what, Natasha?" I asked.

"Well, Brenda has a new girlfriend and *doesn't* need your help *anymore*. So I was wondering, Stuart, can you be *my* road dog? Come on to your camper. I can keep you company."

I was lonely, so I said okay. And Natasha was good company. She could play chess like The Beatles, even better than Brenda was.

"Stuart, you and I will get along fine because I'm *not* a drug addict like Brenda. *I'm an alcoholic like you!*" She saw that I had a bottle of Captain Morgan's spiced rum. "Can I drink with you, Stuart?" she asked.

"Okay, Natasha," I agreed, "I need a drink too!"

So it was not until Saturday afternoon when I knocked on the door of Brenda's apartment. "Brenda, it's Stuart," I announced.

"Hi, Stuart...where have you been? I want you to meet my new girlfriend, Brandy."

"That's okay, Brenda. I'm just seeing that you are okay. Hi, Brandy."

Brandy did not answer me. She was attractive; she had a pretty face.

Brandy finally said to me, "Brenda does *not* need a road dog anymore. *I'll* look out for her from now on!"

"Brenda," I said, "if that's what you want, *it's fine with me.*"

Brenda said, "I know *you love your wife and can never be mine*...so, well, Stuart...I am in love with you if it's any consolation to you, Stuart. And Brandy, *you* won't like me saying this, but Stuart is still and always will be...*my* road dog!"

Now, I still never was sure what a road dog was; but it seemed that soon, *all* the street ladies wanted me to be "their" road dog. When I picked up Natasha to take her to the homeless people's free food places, this time, Natasha had *five* other pretty ladies with her—all working girls from Main Street.

Natasha said to the five girls, "Ladies, this is Stuart. He is a nice guy. Treat him good. He is *our road dog* and can give us rides and check up on us to see that we are okay. And ladies, Stuart likes someone to talk to because he lives in the park!"

The first lady had long blond hair, and looking at her from the back, she appeared to be a young lady. But when you saw her face-to-face, she looked like an old witch, but she had a pleasant personality and was very likeable. Her name was Samantha. And the four other ladies were average-looking ladies.

I said to them, "Listen, ladies...I am a working man, and I'm not around all the time. And I can't promise you anything, but I'd be happy to keep an eye on you *for free*, for Natasha here, if that's okay."

"Thanks, Stuart," said Natasha. "Come with me. Let's get *drunk* together."

As Natasha was spending Saturday night with me in my camper truck, I asked her after drinking some more spiced rum, "Natasha, I don't really know why I'm here with you tonight. I *should be home with my wife*. And how much do I owe you for your companionship?"

"Nothing, Stuart," she replied. "It's free for you. *I just need a friend who cares about what happens to me* and looks after me like you did for Brenda. And Stuart, I have a feeling Brenda will want you back. But until then, and *anytime you need a lady*, come to me, Stuart, okay?"

Sunday I spent *alone* most of the day, sleeping in my camper truck in the park. It was late afternoon, and I had slept all day. But I was awakened by Brenda, *shouting and banging* on my back camper shell door.

"Stuart! Stuart! Wake up! *Wake up!*"

"What is it, Brenda?" I asked in astonishment.

Brenda looked all shook up! I got out and put my arms around her.

"What's the matter, Brenda?" I asked, trying to comfort her.

"There is a killer on the loose!"

"What the heck are you talking about, Brenda?" I asked.

"Stuart, remember my new girlfriend Brandy?" she said.

"Yes, how could I forget?" I stated sadly. "You dumped me for *her!*"

"Somebody murdered my new girlfriend Brandy on Saturday night! She's dead, Stuart!" Brenda was crying bitterly.

"Oh my gosh!" I exclaimed. "I'm so sorry, Brenda!"

"Please stay with me tonight, Stuart. I am so frightened! Maybe the killer *will get me next!* Please stay with me in my motel every chance you get, Stuart...except, of course, when Mr. Roscoe is in town."

"Brenda, why can't *I pay* the rent for you and give you money for your medicine? Or better yet, maybe there is *some kind of help for you.*"

"Well, Stuart," Brenda answered, "Roscoe told me that there is help for heroin addicts, and he says he'll pay for it. It's called a methodone clinic."

"Will it get you off heroin?" I asked, not being familiar with it.

"Yes, it will, Stuart," she said, wiping the tears from her face.

"Brenda, I'm a hopeless alcoholic, but at least I don't do heroin. And if the methodone clinic will help you, then on my next payday, I'll take you and sign you up. Meanwhile, I won't sleep in the park on weekdays anymore, but I'll sleep in a shopping center off of Main Street so you can check in and tell me you are okay. And you will still have your motel room."

Pretty soon, all the ladies on Main Street knew I was sleeping in my camper shell pickup truck at the corner drug store parking lot, and every hour, they would come and knock on my window.

"Hey, Stuart, this is Juanita. Natasha says to tell you hi and thanks for looking out for us and for being *our road dog.*"

"My pleasure, Juanita," I said politely, and I went back to sleep.

Five minutes later, there was banging on my window again, only *loudly*!

"*Help me! Help me!*" a voice screamed.

"Who is it?" I asked.

"It's *Samantha!* Someone *just tried to kill me! I escaped!*"

"Get in here with me quickly!" I urged her.

I held Samantha in my arms, trying to gently calm her down.

"What happened, Samantha?" I asked while holding her.

"I don't remember much because I was loaded and spaced out," she confessed.

"Aren't you always?" I asked realistically.

"Yes, but that's normal for me." Samantha acknowledged quite honestly. "I *think* he was driving a *dark-green van*. He parked in a secluded place about two miles away. And he seemed nice at first, but then he *hit* me and wanted to tie me up! When he went to the back of his van to get some rope, I ran out through the driver's side of his van, and I ran and ran! *Now I'm here with you!*"

Another knock.

"Who is it?" I asked, now a bit frightened myself.

"It's *Brenda!* What's going on?"

"Come in, and we'll tell you!" I said.

I dropped off Brenda and Samantha at the police station so they could tell what they know to the police.

The next day in the newspapers, it said, *"Ten women so far* who worked as prostitutes had been murdered by a *serial killer!"*

A month went by. With no murders, maybe it was safe now! It was December, a rainy Friday night right before Christmas. Brenda needed to get well but *promised* me next Monday she would go to the methadone clinic. My wife was still angry with me. *I couldn't go home.* Samantha stayed with Brenda now at the motel. They shared the room. Natasha was laying low, only dating people she knew and trusted. And the *killer was still on the loose*!

Not many cars were out tonight. Main Street was dark and rainy with a few Christmas lights on in the distance. It was raining *very hard*! There was a knock on my window.

"Hi, it's Brenda. I'm here with Samantha. I'm going to walk with her to see if she gets a date, then *I* have one date lined up with a guy I dated before named Horace, a county worker and a *very nice man*. We will check in with you when we get back, Stuart. But keep your eyes open, just in case!"

"I've got you covered, ladies," I said hero-ically. I had a bottle of spiced rum, and I mixed a glass with soda; I sat in the driver's side, looking into the rainy, dismal, dark night with a good view all the way down Main Street. I *also* had a pair of binoculars that I bought at the flea market. *I was watching them* as their Guardian Angel—their road dog with a halo.

Then, I said a prayer to my Higher Power. "Please protect these two ladies as they go out tonight." Then, another drink of spiced rum. Looking down in the dark and gloomy rainy night, I could see the two ladies clearly.

A van stopped. One lady got in. The van drove away. I put the binoculars down, hearing the sound of rain *pounding on my camper truck cab roof. I was falling asleep!*

"Stuart! Wake up! Let me in! It's Samantha!"

"What's the matter, Samantha?" I asked.

"That's the green van I told you about!" she yelled in a panic. "Brenda got into it! *She's in with the killer!"*

"Are you sure, Samantha?" I asked.

"Yes!" she screamed. "Go *after him, quickly! Go before he gets away!"*

I turned the engine on and *stepped on the gas* and *peeled out* of the *parking lot.* I could see the van's taillights off in the distance. I hadn't followed taillights in a long time, but I was very *good at it!*

Suddenly, a police car was behind us and was *flashing his lights and following me!*

I stopped and shouted, "Get out, Samantha! Wave the cop car down and *take him* to the *same place* the killer took you! I'll follow the van. *Brenda is in there!"*

Samantha stood right in the middle of Main Street in the rain, frantically waving her hands! The cop car stopped. Samantha got in. *"That's the serial killer!"* she screamed.

"In the pickup truck?" the patrolman asked.

"No! No! No!" she yelled. "That's *Brenda's road dog, Stuart. He* is following the killer, who is driving a green van! And, Mr. Cop, I think I know where the van is going because *I'm the one* he tried to kill before! I *know* where he's going!"

"Calm down, lady," the police officer said. "I'll call for some back up, and you can take us there!"

Luckily for me, the killer was driving on side roads. In the dark pounding rain, it reminded me of driving in snowstorms back in New Jersey. I turned off my headlights because it was 2:00 a.m., and nobody was on the roads now. And I didn't want the killer to see me following him.

I was following his taillights in the dark, like in a snowstorm back in New Jersey. I had no idea where I was or where I was going, but now, I could tell I was in the woods somewhere.

I saw the van stop, and its lights went off. I knew I needed another drink. I finished off the bottle of spiced rum. If ever I needed Dutch courage, *I needed it now*! I had no weapons in the camper, only a black plastic garbage bag. I wore it as a raincoat.

I parked one hundred yards away and walked in the dark wet, rainy woods toward the killer's van. I reached down and conveniently found a stick that looked like an Irish shillelagh. I heard struggling in the van. It was still raining, but rain was being filtered by the tree.

"Hey, Horace!" I shouted loudly. "I know what your game is, Horace! I'm Brenda's road dog! You know I'm nobody to mess with! *So let her go now!*"

"Yes," Brenda said, "my road dog Stuart is seven feet tall and carries two guns! He'll blow your head off, and you'll never get out of here alive! You better do what my road dog says, Horace!"

"Both guns are aimed at you, Horace!" I warned him. "Let her go! Get out of the van! All I want is Brenda! Then I'll let you go!"

Horace got out of the van with a rope in his hands. It was dark and rainy.

"Drop the rope and put your hands on the van!" I shouted.

Suddenly, Horace realized that I was not seven feet tall and that I did not have a gun. But what he *did not know was that my stick was a shillelagh-type weapon, and I knew how to use it*, and, from my boxing days, how to box!

And as Horace attacked me with his knife and rope, I distracted him with my left punch, and with my right hand, I held the angled end of my stick and hit him on the back of his head and knocked him out *cold!*

Just then, several police cars arrived with lights flashing. Samantha had brought the police to help. Brenda came over to me and hugged me tight and kissed me. "Thanks, *my road dog!*" she said.

Horace was taken away by the police. And so it was that he was indeed the serial killer.

Next Monday morning, Brenda went to the Methadone Clinic. It nearly cost me my entire paycheck. But Brenda said she needed to chip, or still use drugs, only *less* than before. So now she was doing Methadone *and* heroin—*both*!

I went back to sleeping in the park during the daytime Mondays through Fridays. I always phoned my wife.

"What's new, Stuart?" Maria would ask.

"Nothing at all, dear," I said, not wanting my dear wife to worry.

"I miss you, Maria, and I want to come home soon," I said.

"If you're still drinking, Stuart, the answer is *no*!"

It was Saturday morning again. I went to check up on Brenda at her motel room.

"Well, Brenda...good thing with that serial killer that I was *drunk*. If I had been sober, then something like that would have *really scared me*!"

"Me too!" she said. "I was high on drugs!"

We both laughed.

"Hey Stuart," she suggested, "Why don't you try what I'm doing? I'll *fix* you a needle..."

By now, I was in a trance. Instead of Brenda looking like a princess, *she looks like a pretty angel, all right*, but a pretty *angel of death*!

I blacked out into oblivion.

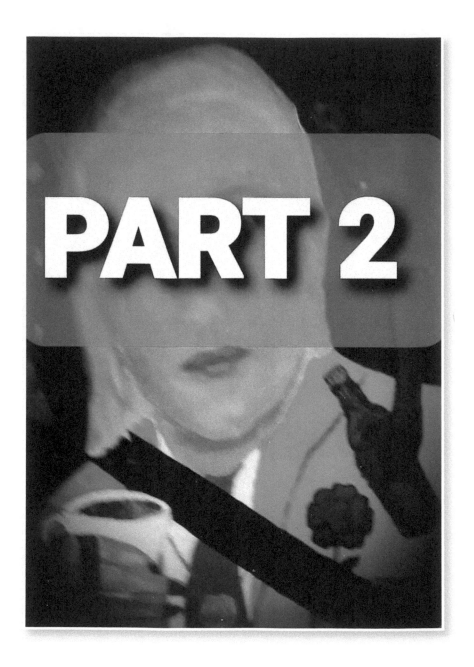

CHAPTER TWENTY

Get Sober or Die!

Now I was an alcoholic using heroin too—*again!* I was homeless, living in the back of a pickup truck with campershell on it. Alcohol and heroin was a *deadly* combination.

I was drinking obsessively—I could not stop. My pavement princess, Brenda, gave me watered-down heroin. I couldn't look. She put the needle in my arm. The world around started spinning, and I felt like I was in a coma-tose deadly dreamlike state. And I instinctively also knew that *if I lay down, I would die.* But I worked a midnight shift in Los Angeles, and it was around 9:00 p.m. I had to go to work. In a drug-induced rage, I yelled at Brenda! Then I had the "gift of desperation."

I called my *wife,* Maria, for help. I was in a drunken dreamlike state. Brenda locked me out of her apartment. I was alone. Maria thought I would be dead soon.

Maria said yes. She was on the way. She would come and help me. Maria told me when she was driving me to work that she heard of a treatment program at a behavior medical center. She said my insurance at my midnight-shift job would probably cover it. I was desperate for help but knew in my heart and mind that it would never work because it seemed like all they wanted was money. But if I still was alive in the morning, I would check it out.

The next morning, they said, "Yes, you are a heroin addict and an alcoholic, and first we must detox you. We will give you something that will knock you out for a while so you can detox."

Wow, it sounded good to me. I needed a rest. So I signed tip willingly so I could be knocked out for a few days. That is why I went in. That was April 1992.

I was still there, knocked out, in and out of consciousness, and I was still not convinced that anyone or anything could help me with my chemical dependency addiction problems. I heard someone say they were a care unit. They cared as long as you have money. Then, they didn't care anymore.

There was one counselor there I liked—a very sharp guy who was teaching a class about recovery. And he said something I just could not believe. He stood in front of my group and told us something incredible. He said he was just like us, a fellow alcoholic and drug addict, and that he had not taken even one drink or used one drug in more than two and a half years. I did not and could not believe him.

He said, "I did it by going to twelve-step meetings, and you are going to go too!"

I was put in a van with a bunch of other guys that night. The driver was a volunteer with four years of sobriety. We were whisked away into the foggy night. He played songs he liked on the radio, but soon we arrived at a church parking lot that was already full of cars.

So our van parked. About ten men, including me, from our treatment center got out. We went inside the church where an AA meeting was being held. I was afraid, and it was very strange. And at first, I felt like I did *not* belong there. I wanted to leave. The last thing I wanted was to be preached to in a church.

But I was quickly assured that this twelve-step program was not a church service and that its only members were addicts and alcoholics and that their program worked by one alcoholic or addict talking to another.

There were about at least two hundred people at the meeting that night—ladies and men all looking well-dressed, all neat and clean. Most of the people did not look like alcoholics in my mind, but a few did.

All of a sudden, panic set in. A sexy-looking, very pretty lady was walking toward me. She said to me, "Hi! You must be new. My name is Dolores!" Then she shocked me by giving me a big hug and seductively said, "Keep coming back!"

I retreated to the back of the room, looking like a deer caught in the headlights. Before I could recover from Dolores, another lady named Cathy came over and introduced herself and also gave me a hug and told me to keep coming back. She told me something very incredible too—that she had six years of sobriety and that I could do it also, "one day at a time." Such was my introduction to twelve-step meetings, which I shall never forget. I suddenly wanted what those ladies had—to be sober!

Coffee and cookies were available for free, and the meeting that night was a *speaker meeting*. The meeting format was two ten-minute speakers, a coffee break, then a forty-five-minute main speaker. Basically, the talks were about people who had recovered from alcohol and drugs. They talked about what it used to be like, what happened, and what it was like now.

Everything at that first meeting was a blur, but an amazing thing happened. I began to believe and have hope. I thought, *Maybe a person really can get clean and sober!*

So many people saying they were clean and sober couldn't all be lying. So I kept on going to daily treatments, where I lived for the twenty-eight days. They taught me that alcoholism was a disease and just maybe I had it. And I finally knew what was wrong with me, and it was also called chemical dependency. And it was not my fault. I was not responsible for my disease, but now I knew there was a way out. I was responsible for my recovery.

So I was still in the treatment facility, going to meetings every day, both at AA and NA. Since I'd tried heroin, I thought I'd better go to NA also, and I did. And in the rooms of Narcotics Anonymous, I heard an important message that I shall never forget that saved my life. In one of NA's readings, they stated, "Make no mistake about this: alcohol is a drug!" Both programs helped me never to pick up the first drink or drug ever again.

After twenty days of being in meetings and recovery, I was getting very excited. I now knew what had been wrong with me for the past thirty years. I was an alcoholic. I had a disease of chemical dependency. All I had to do was not drink or use one day at a time. Because of listening in NA meetings, I heard people staying clean fifteen years or more, even from tough drugs like heroin. This seemed too good to be true. There was a way out of the insanity of chemical dependency. *I must share this with everyone I can.* My thoughts went to Brenda, who was undoubtedly in her motel room shooting up right now! So that night, I was thinking that she might die soon if I didn't tell her.

She would believe me if I told her. So I was so obsessed with carrying the message of recovery. I went AWOL and jumped over the wall of the recovery house. I went to Brenda's motel room at around 11:00 p.m. and pounded on the door.

"I've got to speak with you! Open the door! It's important!"

So when she finally showed her face and opened the door, I could tell that some guy in the background of her apartment was hiding. Brenda opened the door but left the safety chain on, and I told her, "Hey, Brenda, I just wanted to tell you, you never have to use drugs or drink again. I found a way to stop. I have found a way out. And you know me, Brenda, that I would never lie to you, especially about something like this!"

CHAPTER TWENTY-ONE

"Slow-Briety"
Just Don't Drink!

I successfully completed the twenty-eight-day
program at Chemical Dependency Treatment

Center, and the *first* lesson was places like long-term live-in recovery programs and even jails and prisons *could save your life* because for a real chemically dependent person, the *hardest part was to stop drinking or using!* Most people just couldn't stop.

The *second* message emphasized was suggest to them to go to twelve-step meetings since you could not "tell" an addictive person to do anything (as they wouldn't do it, then).

They *suggested* that after the treatment program, we went to *ninety meetings in ninety days*. Why? Because *recovery programs* and *jails could get you sober*, but I needed to go to twelve-step meetings? Why? *Because they worked!*

So *going to twelve-step meetings kept you sober!* I did my ninety meetings in ninety days, and *more*. After going to meetings every day for a while, I was "overwhelmed" with my *new life* in twelve-step programs. I *loved* recovery!

The *God* word no longer scared me as I was told I could choose *my own conception of God, or not*—it was *not* a requirement for twelve-steps. A *"higher power"* was suggested—some power *greater than myself*, just *not me*.

After all, *my own very best thinking got me drunk*, so it was suggested that I got a sponsor. Someone in the twelve-step program with *long-term sobriety* was preferred. So one day at a time, I went to a meeting because I had, in the past, drunk alcohol every day.

I was told *I needed a replacement* for that drink, and that replacement was to *go to a meeting every day*!

I was here to tell you that twelve-step meetings worked for me. Yes! The meetings had *strange power* for me. Before the meeting, I was really squirrely. *I wanted a drink badly*! At a regular twelve-step meeting, everyone got good therapy—a chance to share without being interrupted as no cross talk was allowed.

A twelve-step meeting went like this. One person talked about how they got sober, telling three things: (1) what it used to be like, (2) what happened to get them sober, and (3) what sobriety was like for them today. An hour of such testimony had a positive effect.

After the twelve-step meeting and sharing with the group, *my desire for a drink was gone like magic*! It worked! And I had no idea why. But the bottom line was that *it worked* when nothing else I ever tried before did.

GOD at first meant to me "Group of Drunks" because others knew secrets and coping skills on how to live a *happy, sober life*. In addition to just not drinking, twelve-step meetings helped me face *life on life's terms*. I always "ran away" from responsibility and *emotions* before by *putting my brain to sleep with alcohol* because I did not know how to deal with *people*, *places*, and *things* while sober.

GOD also meant Good Orderly Direction. That meant instead of everything in the world being a mess, the opposite was true if looked at from a different perspective, <u>that everything</u> in the universe was wonderful and for reasons unknown, everything *was exactly the way it was supposed to be at the moment*. Why? Because *the Higher Power*, GOD, did *not* make *any mistakes*!

Most all of the ideas in the twelve-step program worked for me. At meetings, it was suggested that I took what I needed and discarded the rest. I learned that *not* going to meetings was *not being sober*. For a real alcoholic like me, it was called being a "dry drunk" because you still have no way to deal with life's ups and downs. So going to meetings daily was a *must for me to do*.

Dolores was happy to see me back at the speaker's Thursday night meeting again. I got there late this night, and it was "standing room" only, except there was only *one open seat next to Dolores*! Usually her husband sat there.

Up at the podium, a well-groomed man was introduced as tonight's twelve-step main speaker. The speaker said, "Welcome, *newcomers*. As you know, *us alcoholics are all liars, cheats, and thieves*, but *we don't do it as much anymore*. We don't change *overnight*. *We are not saints!* If you were a horse thief before, now you're a *sober horse thief.* But the good news is that over time, your ideas of *good* will *win* over your old ideas of bad. It's simple: daily constant contact with your Higher Power, and simply *do what you are supposed to do.* You and your Higher Power knows what that is. It's a simple program for complicated people. Don't drink and go to meetings! You never have to take another drink as long as you live if you don't want to!"

Now *that* was great information!

What a great meeting, I was thinking.

Then, he said, "Yes, we are *all former liars, cheats, and thieves!* In this very room, there are people *who have recovered* from this seem-ingly *hopeless disease* of addiction. *People who are former murderers, prostitutes, ex-of-fenders, bank robbers, and more—you name it, and we are here in this room! All of us are former gutter drunks, just like you!* Before com-ing to twelve-step meetings, we ruined our lives and our families' lives and everyone around us because we were self-centered. But now we have changed and have over time become *good* people!"

"We *now* have found *a new sober way of life,*" he added. "And *today,* we are *respected members of society.* And yes, we are the ones who want to *help you and guide you into your new life!*"

How ironic and crazy, I thought!

After that meeting, it seemed like we, *in recovery*, were a bunch of *misfits* who banded together for one purpose—not to drink or use any mind-altering drugs, including *the drug alcohol, just for today!* One day at a time.

I started working on the twelve steps:

Step 1: I admitted I was powerless over my addiction and that my life had become *unmanageable*.

Step 2: I came to believe that a power greater than myself could restore me to *sanity*. *Wow!* Did that mean all this time I was insane? Yes! Drinking against *my own free will and not being able to stop was as crazy as it got!* Doing things I'd never do, if sober, *was insanity too!* Yes! I did believe a power greater than myself could get my sanity back by helping me, one day at a time, *not* to pick up that *first* drink! One drink *would* trigger the obsession and craving *again*, and then, even a thousand drinks wouldn't be enough. The craving was never satisfied *until your dead!*

Step 3: I made a decision to turn our will and our lives over to this Higher Power, God, as we understood him (or her). Wow, how did I know *what God's will* was and what my will was? I heard at a meeting *prayer or even wishing real hard* was actually *talking to God* (or whatever *you* want to call *your Higher Power)*, and *meditation* was *listening* to God (your

Higher Power). Basically, deep inside you, your inner voice of "do the right thing" would override immediate gratification desires. "Do what you are supposed to be doing—*you* and *your Higher Power know* what that is."

After those first three steps, I was feeling like *I* was a true *twelve-step guru now!* There were *twelve steps;* I only worked three. But the rest of the steps could wait, I thought, as I went out to the streets again to try to help others, which was step 12. I was ready to save the world from alcoholism!

Step 12: Having had a spiritual awakening as a result of these steps, we *tried* to carry the message of recovery to others. Well, I had a Higher Power now that I had *invented*, and it was working for me! And then one day, I saw a drunken bum dressed in rags lying in front of the lawn of a fast-food restaurant—empty beer cans all around him.

I tried to give him some AA (Alcoholics Anonymous) literature and see if I could help him. He was still half drunk and was *very insulted by me for even suggesting that he had a "drinking problem."*

"How dare you insinuate that I'm an alcoholic?" he answered angrily, slurring his words.

I told him where a meeting was and that it was *free!* Also, that they had *free coffee*, and maybe even *cookies!*

"*Free?*" he said. "*Cookies too?*" He thought about it for a moment. "Yes, okay...thanks... maybe I will check it out. *I'm hungry!*"

Six months later, I was at a meeting. A fellow walked up to me. He was all neat and clean. He said, "Hey, remember *me*?"

I said, "I'm not sure. After all, I meet a lot of people."

"I am the guy you spoke to in front of the fast-food place. I went to meetings like you said and got *more* than *free* coffee and cookies! I've been sober ever since!"

He now was back with his family and had a job. Not only did I get to stay sober, but I learned that I could help others too! It felt good!

Back at my *regular* Thursday night speaker meeting now, my seat was *always next to Dolores*, who, since I had known her, had had more than six years of sobriety. That was like *incredible* to me, now with *only* nine months of being sober. Maybe, I would get my *nine-month chip tonight.*

But this night, Dolores was all dressed up—even prettier than usual—and she was wearing a *low-cut dress*. She asked me, "Stuart, I'm celebrating seven years of sobriety tonight. Can *you* give me my *seven-year cake*?"

Wow! What an honor!

"I'd love to, Dolores. It's an honor! Sure!" I said.

There was another interesting thing about twelve-step meetings that I went to. In the first year, at some meetings, they handed out *free* keychain tokens called "chips." Sometimes they were made out of plastic and sometimes out of metal. They celebrated the number of days a person stayed sober. When I was new, and even today, I loved "chip" meetings because everyone who took a chip or a birthday cake had to say to everyone how they managed to stay sober that long.

Birthdays in twelve-step programs were celebrated after a person was sober for a year or more (including weekends). Being sober meant not taking alcohol or anything else that affected you *from the neck up.*

Dolores also had been chosen by the group that night to be the "chip chick." As such, *she* would pass out the chips. That was why she chose me to give her her sobriety cake—because she could not give it to herself. But now there was another reason—she had a secret!

Dolores was passing out sobriety chips, giving each recipient a chip and a *hug*. Then, it was my turn! "Let's hear it for *Stuart*, with *nine months of sobriety! One day at a time!*" Dolores said to the group.

Everyone was cheering. "Yeah, Stuart!" said *Dolores*. Now I had to tell the group *how I did it.*

But first, Dolores surprised me by *kissing me right on my lips in front of three hundred people!*

That's weird, I thought. Something was strange about her kiss too. Although I enjoyed the kiss, I was at the same time very embarrassed and shy. I turned *beet red.* I was at the podium now.

"Hello, I'm Stuart. I'm sober because of my Higher Power, going to meetings, and not picking up a drink...one day at a time! Thank you for my nine-month chip."

Then, I sat down. I knew now it was my turn to give Dolores her seven-year cake. Soon thereafter, *Dolores's* name was called, and someone in the back of the room handed me a *large flat-pan birthday cake.* And it was *heavy* because there were a lot of people at this big meeting to feed cake to. The meeting needed a very *big cake,* and it was decorated with the number seven on it. And seven *lighted* candles were on top. It seemed like I walked a half mile just to get to the front of the room. I held the cake out to Dolores, and she blew the candles out in my direction. I felt warm air.

As the breeze from the candle blowing blew by, I noticed *something* was not right, even though she succeeded in blowing all of the candles out.

Then it dawned on me. *I could smell alcohol on her breath!* Just then, I *snapped*—a moment of weakness! I *dropped her cake on the floor* and instinctively French-kissed her—not really because of her but I was trying to get a taste of alcohol off her tongue!

Then, I realized what I was doing, pulled myself together, and said to her calmly, "Congratulations, Dolores, *I'm proud of you!*"

Dolores was happy and said to me that she had not been kissed *that good* ever before and also happy that I did not *reveal* what her little "secret" was, that she'd been drinking and had *blown off her sobriety.* Her husband got loaded and left her.

After the meeting was over, I told Dolores, "Hey, Dolores, is there *anything* I can do for you? If so, please let me know. *When you are ready to start your recovery over* or go to a meeting, *just call me.*"

"Okay," said Dolores, "*thanks, Stuart.* I'm going away to Las Vegas for two years. I'll call you when I come back." She gave me her phone number. And it was two years that went by until Dolores called me up on the phone. "Stuart, I'm ready. Take me to a meeting." She picked me up in her new car and had been sober ever since!

Dolores drove away in a *brand-new* Mercedes automobile.

"Hey, Stuart," someone asked. "Do you have any idea who *that lady is?*"

"No," I answered, "but I certainly like her and hope *she stays sober.*"

Dolores was really a very famous adult movie actress whose stage name was Doris the Doll Face I was told.

"You're kidding me!" I said. "I've seen all of her movies! *I thought she looked familiar.* You're right. That is *her!*"

Back at home with my wife, Maria, for a little while, I still was set on *helping everyone I meet and know*, who was out there *dying* from alcohol and drugs, to get into recovery. It was my new purpose in life—helping others.

I realized that neither I nor my family was ready for me to return home and that just being sober and working only *three* of the *twelve-steps was not enough*!

It was clear that I needed more recovery. I was still a sick man.

Step 4 was for me to "make a searching and fearless moral inventory of myself," and *step 5* of the twelve steps suggested that I "admit to God, to myself, and to another human being the exact nature of my wrongs."

It was extremely hard for an alcoholic like me to *ever* admit that I was *wrong* about *any-thing*! I was still living in a camper shell pickup truck. I heard at a meeting, "Our problems are of our own making." And yes, I created this one. I went back to live in my pickup truck with a camper shell on it, but this time, the truck was parked at meetings all day and all night. And I went to *lots* of meetings—every day!

I had heard there was a "good" twelve-step meeting at a church right by the park that I used to sleep in by day, and still did. It was a *Friday Night twelve-step meeting.*

I had just slept in the park all day this Friday, and that meeting was nearby. I'd never been to this particular meeting before. I did not know anyone there. I went into this new meeting not knowing what to expect.

I told the meeting leader that I had nine months of sobriety. I was new to this meeting, and the leader of the meeting read the twelve-step readings and then told the thirty people in the room, "We have a *new member* of our group tonight. Here is Stuart, with *nine months* of sobriety."

The group replied in unison, "Hi, Stuart!"

The leader then looked at me and said, "Welcome, Stuart, to the Friday Night *Gay and Lesbian meeting!*"

Gay and lesbian meeting? I was thinking. "Oh, no! What will people think if they see me in here?" I mumbled.

The guy next to me replied, "Stuart, it's okay. They already *know!*"

"Know what?" I asked trepidatiously.

"That *you* are an *alcoholic!*" he answered,

"You are right!" I said in confidence.

"I'm Jo C. I have seven years of sobriety. So you have nine months of sobriety?"

"Yes, I do," I admitted.

"Do you have a *sponsor*?" Jo C. asked me.

"*No, Jo C., I don't,*" I said.

"Well, you *do* now!" Jo C. said proudly.

"I do?" I asked him.

"Yes," he replied. "Do you have a service commitment?"

"No," I said.

"Okay," Jo C. told me, "from tonight on, you are our Friday night coffee person!"

"What do I do?" I asked, wondering.

"Well, you will show up here early every Friday and make coffee for the meeting, and then *clean up afterwards!*" Jo C. said. "It will help you *stay sober*, Stuart. *If you don't want to relapse, do as I say!*"

"Okay, Jo C.," I agreed.

So Jo C. became my first twelve-step sponsor. At the end of the meeting, the *leader* was thanking everyone who participated in the meeting. And Jo C. volunteered to the group. "Let's *welcome* our *newest group member*, Stuart, with over nine months of sobriety. And Stuart has volunteered to be our new coffee person for *the next year!*"

I did?

So that Friday night, the group loaded a big, giant coffee-making machine in my camper with coffee supplies. Now, I had originally *never intended to go back to that meeting* again, but now, I kept my coffee commitment for a year.

I told Jo C. that I had lost my job and family and was homeless again.

Jo C., my sponsor, told me, "Stuart, God does not make any mistakes! You are *exactly where you are supposed to be in your recovery process right now!* It's part of a new and better plan! God took you down so he could work on you. Now you can attend even *more twelve-step meetings!*"

"You are right, Jo C.!" I said.

And exactly that I did. I got more service commitments at other meetings, and my sobriety was getting better and stronger.

By networking at meetings, I heard that the State of California had a program to help recovering alcoholics go back to college, so I signed up. And being sober, I became more aware of my surroundings and attended a homeless outreach program for veterans. Since I *qualified as a homeless veteran*, I was put on a waiting list for veterans' housing to get a place to stay of my own.

Now in sobriety, things were truly *getting better*.

CHAPTER TWENTY-TWO

Sober
You Can Do Anything!

Now, after I became homeless again, Brenda disappeared for *some* reason. She *avoided* me at all costs.

Finally, I was on speaking terms with my dear wife, Maria, again, and I started to attend a junior college once more. This time, I was *sober in college*.

I had been told in the twenty-eight-day rehab program that I had chemical psychosis and "wet brain" and was headed toward dementia because of past drinking and using. And in early sobriety, I always, for the longest time, had a "poisoned headache" consisting of a very dark feeling on my brain that would *not go away!*

In twelve-step AA meetings, a "longtimer" was a person who had over thirty years of sobriety. At one of my meetings, I spoke with a longtimer.

He said, "Yes, I know what you are talking about, and it usually takes about *five years* for your *brain to heal itself from the damage alcohol and drugs cause*."

And apparently, the longtimer was right. I heard this event expressed in several ways *in AA meetings*. What was said was, "Well, it takes about five years for the *fog* to lift out of your brain!"

In NA meetings, this was said: "Well, if you can stay clean for five years or more, your head will pop out of your ass!" Same event, different ways to say it. The common denominator of both would be to stay *clean and sober*!

I was accepted again to college. So now I was in Roadrunner Junior College. This time, my main motive was just wanting my damaged brain to *heal itself*, and I studied *day and night just to learn*! I thought that I would fail everything! But I was determined to *try* to learn *anything* they put in front of me *just to get my mind back*!

To my surprise and everyone else's surprise, my grades this time were *straight As*. The state-sponsored agency had prophesied wrongly that I would fail. (I found that out later.)

I kept going to meetings and, at college each semester, made the dean's list with straight As. However, it did not come easy. I also got a job at the veterans' hospital and obtained *housing* for veterans. I worked four to five hours, "weed-whacking" at a national veterans' cemetery. I was studying to be an alcohol and drug counselor.

I got an unpaid internship at Cedarwood Twenty-Eight-Day Chemical Dependency Center. I had over two years of sobriety by that time, and now it was my turn to give back.

I told the newcomers, "Hey, I have over two years sobriety. I'm taking you to meetings, 'cause it works!"

At the same time, I also studied to obtain an AA degree in *human services*. In 1995, I graduated with honors, and to my surprise, I got a letter from *Who's Who in America's Junior Colleges* announcing that I was one of the five students selected to be included in their book this year! I stared at the form! I did not know what to write. I only tried to stay sober and learn. I did not even think of the grades.

With a certificate of alcohol and drug studies and an associate of arts degree in human services, I had learned a lot about chemical dependency that drinking alcohol excessively causes lots of diseases. One professor told us that the dendrites of our brain cells were like little tree roots and alcohol shriveled up these dendrites and destroyed connections of dendrites between cells, causing brain damage, and communication was lost, killing brain cells! That feeling of euphoria when drunk was *actually* the feeling of *brain cells dying!* The professor said also, "That is why when we die, we are at peace and see a white light. It's your brain cells all dying!"

Wow! I thought. We think we will return to our sober normal self in the morning, but the professor told us that was not always the case because over time, we will get wet brain and be stuck on stupid with *dementia!*

At Roadrunner Junior College's alcohol and drug studies program, I learned about the big mysteries when I had been drinking. For example, I learned that one can of beer, one glass of wine, one shot glass of whiskey were each a legal dose of the *drug* alcohol and that the type of drug alcohol was a depressant drug and being drunk was a drug *overdose*.

Wow! When I was drinking and felt depressed, I drank a depressant, and after killing my brain cells and the effects wore off, I was now even *more* depressed! I was glad I was sober now!

Also, I learned even more that a blackout meant my mind was functioning only in "short-term memory," with an average memory frame about twenty minutes. This time frame was moving forward with the clock, and drinking enough alcohol had anesthetized, or put to sleep, and shut down my ability to store information into my long-term memory. As a result, I couldn't remember anything of what happened past twenty minutes ago, such as where I parked my car, how I got where I am, who I was with, or what I did past those twenty minutes. Most of the time, I could not remember the night before at all after a few drinks bunched up in an hour's time!

When I had been drinking, I had no idea of the real insanity of how I had been drinking myself into oblivion!

I learned that the liver in my body could only process and get rid of a one-ounce dose of alcohol per hour. (The following statements are just for examples.) When I drank more in that hour's time frame, my brain and body started to be negatively affected.

When I drank two drinks in one hour, there was relaxation and loss of motor control of my body. When I drank three drinks in one hour, I started to lose all inhibitions and act out on ideas. I lost emotional control, with violent rages to hysteria resulting. Short-term memory would start to take over.

When I drank four drinks in one hour, my body started to save me. I began throwing up! The body wanted to get rid of the alcohol, even when I *didn't!* Motor functions failed, including slurring speech, the inability to walk or stand straight, walking with "rubbery legs," etc.

When I drank five drinks of a legal dose of alcohol, my brain tried to save my life by shutting the body down, and I would *pass out!* I remembered all these from personal experience!

Now, if you drank *more* than this amount before you pass out, the alcohol could *kill you!* And here was why: because the next thing your brain would do was to shut down your heart and cause you to stop breathing! Make no mistake. *Too much alcohol in a short time could and would kill you!* I realized how lucky I was to still be alive!

Self-knowledge with a degree in alcohol and drug studies, together with my twelve-step meeting knowledge, was the way I could now help others in every way to stay clean and sober. But *what about helping my family?*

At Roadrunner Junior College, I took a class which told me that alcoholism was a family disease and I was not the only one that was sick. Not only did my drinking behavior cause my whole family to be forced to develop coping skills just to cope with *me* and not only had I messed up my own life, but I messed up my family's life too!

My wife, Maria, was trying to be a good wife, but she had no idea that she enabled me to keep drinking when she bought booze for me. Instead of taking care of herself and her needs, she always was worried about me. I was not there for my daughter either. But the real message to me was that *I caused my family's dysfunction!* Now, *it was up to me to help fix it!*

I was sober now for four years. At one meeting, I was inspired by a motorcycle guy named Bill, who had two more years of sobriety than I did. He already finished junior college and was now going to California State University. Well, if Bill could do it, so could I!

So the next thing I knew, I was back in *school* attending Cal State, majoring in psychology. As an undergrad, I helped start twelve-step meetings on the college campus. I was surprised how many students and even college professors and other faculty were members of the twelve-step group.

I met lots of new friends there—both men and women at that college meeting, including a red-haired lady named Mindy. I had veterans' supported housing now—my own place. Maria and my family had doubts at first about my steadfast determination to finish college. However, in June 1998, I graduated Cal State with honors, having earned a bachelor of arts degree in psychology. Just by coincidence, my daughter, Myra, was graduating Cal State the same weekend I was, with a bachelor of science degree in science.

All dressed up in my graduation cap and gown, my hat had a twelve-step meeting *symbol* on the top of it in white tape for all to see, but probably only others in a twelve-step program would know what it meant. But to my surprise, across the stadium in the crowd, some lady had the same logo as I did on her own hat!

Myra had taped a frog on *her* hat. It was a happy, magical time. My family was proud of me and Myra. That weekend, everyone in my family was speaking to me. Observing my graduation photos with my family was my college twelve-step meeting friend, Mindy. Mindy had eight years of sobriety and was only *two courses* away from getting her bachelor's degree. Mindy volunteered to snap photos of my family all together. (Later on, Mindy met some guy and relapsed on drugs and alcohol. She never did graduate.)

Now, I was a college graduate with a bachelor of arts degree in psychology. But *Bill* had gone on to get *his master's degree!* Well, if Bill could do it, *so could I!* Soon, the very next semester, I was accepted and was *going for my master's degree!* I was sober, still going to meetings, and still an honor student. *I was on a roll, so why stop?*

Then, one day out of the blue, I got a call from Brenda! She wanted to see me. I asked her, "Why?"

"Because I want to *stop using drugs!* I need your help *badly*, Stuart," she confessed. "I'm tired, Stuart! Please help me!"

So in between classes and on weekends, I saw Brenda. She looked pretty beat up now.

Brenda's Intervention

Back in my drinking days when I was Brenda's road dog, Brenda *always* had hair under her armpits, but I noticed now that the underarm hair was gone.

I was clean and sober about seven years now. I told Brenda, "I was always ready to help you. Where did you go?"

"Well, Stuart," she replied, "I loved you, and I knew that if I stayed around you, I'd be *nothing but trouble* for you and *I'd bring you down!*

It's *because* I cared about you that *I stayed away!* My life is a total *wreck,* Stuart! I couldn't stop using heroin."

"Well, Brenda," I asked, "*will* you go to rehab? That is, if I can get you in there?"

"Yes!" she said.

"Will you go to twelve-step meetings?" I asked.

"Of course!" she answered.

"Brenda, I'll pick you up for a meeting *tonight* at six."

However, when I went to get Brenda, she was not there. So I went on with my college work, and after a month passed by, I got a call. It was Brenda again.

"Sorry Stuart," she began. "I'm an addict! *I can't stop using!* I need help!"

"Listen, Brenda," I said sternly. "*Unless you're serious about getting clean, I cannot help you!* Call me only when you *are ready!*"

"I want your help *now!*" she insisted.

The next Saturday morning, I took Brenda out for breakfast and told her, "I know how *hard it is to get clean and sober.* And the only way I will help you is that *you agree and give me your permission to do whatever it takes to get you into rehab. Only then will I help you!*"

So Brenda agreed in writing that I was at liberty to do *whatever it took* to get her into a twenty-eight-day twelve-step recovery and drug treatment program. I also told Brenda,

"When you get clean, grow your underarm hair back for me...I like it!"

She agreed. But she *did not really believe* that she would or ever could *ever* go to rehab. And she just *could not stop using heroin and methadone every day.*

But Brenda had found GOD now called a "Gift of Desperation"! There was hope for her!

I had *no idea how* I could get her into rehab. But one day in the town newspaper, I saw an article about street girls, and featured in this article was *an interview with Brenda* with her photo! She had told on herself about her life on the street to the newspapers!

Remembering my promise to Brenda that "I'd do *whatever it took,*" I sent a copy of that article to Brenda's mother, who really did not know what Brenda was up to.

When Brenda found out what I had done, she was *furious*! And she sent a large man into the park to *beat me up.* But I was driving my yellow car then, and I drove away fast, locking my car doors, being followed by Brenda and this large guy. I pulled into a shopping center with Brenda and this guy in another car following me. I ran into a department store for safety—in fear of my life.

This guy was still waiting outside to beat me up! So I called the police. *Then, I noticed my car moving!* Brenda and this man had just *stolen* my yellow car and *drove it away!*

So now, *my car* was gone, and *Brenda* stole it! I reported her to the police. Next day, the police called me, saying that a police helicopter flew over the area and they spotted my yellow car about ten blocks away from where it was stolen.

Brenda had been in jails and prisons many times before, and now because of her stealing my car, Brenda *was about to be sent back to prison again!*

So I went to see Brenda in jail and told her, "Brenda, *don't worry! I'll get you out!*"

"Why did you do this to me, Stuart?" Brenda asked with tears running down her cheeks.

"Brenda," I said, "*remember you gave me permission* to do *whatever it took* to get you into rehab?"

"Yes, I remember," she cried.

"Well, Brenda," I continued, "*this is what it takes!* I've done an *intervention on you!* You've never in your life been in rehab before. I've arranged it with the court. *You have two choices: go with me and let me take you to rehab or go to prison!*"

Because of *my good reputation* as an honor student, the court released Brenda from jail after she had been in there for *three months* into *my custody* under one *condition:* that I take her *immediately and directly* to the *Squeaky Clean Rehab Center for Women!*

But there was one quick stop she needed to make, and that was to go to the town's Social Security Office first on the way and pick up her Social Security card, which was ready for her. She needed the card for *admittance* into the rehab center.

As I parked in front of the Social Security Office building, *Brenda* got out; *but instead* of going into the Social Security Office, to my shock and surprise, Brenda *ran away across the street* to a creepy old guy who was waiting for her! Oh no! It was Roscoe!

"What are you doing, Brenda?" I shouted in horror.

"I'll be back, Stuart. I need a fix!"

Well, it was getting late now. But someone I knew from a twelve-step meeting came by, and I told him what happened.

"Brenda was released from the court into my custody," I explained. "What can I do now?"

My AA friend said, "Just *trust in your Higher Power*. And *never give up five minutes before the miracle happens*!"

Just as I was about to give up completely, Brenda came back, got her Social Security card, and said, "Take me to rehab, Stuart. I'm *ready now*!"

Brenda went to the Squeaky Clean Rehab Center for Women. After about three months later, Brenda's mother, father, and sisters all went to visit Brenda at the Squeaky Clean

Rehab Center. They could not believe how nice Brenda was recovering as if she were a brand-new person!

Brenda took me aside at the Rehab Center and told me, "Thanks, Stuart. You saved my life!" Then, she lifted up her arm and showed underarm hair. "I have ninety days!" she said.

Brenda's mother told me, "Stuart, it's a *miracle! We never thought we would ever see the day when Brenda got off drugs! Thank you, Stuart!*"

Brenda got clean and went to twelve-step meetings. I went on and completed graduate school with honors and earned my master's degree at Cal State University in the year 2000.

I was eight years sober. On my ninth year to the day of my "twelve-step *sobriety* birthday," I was offered my dream job in a *large office.*

Sobriety worked!

CHAPTER TWENTY-THREE

Running Toward Relapse

Thanks to my sobriety and twelve-step meetings, finally after ten long years of living away
from my wife's home, I was now a univer-

sity-level college graduate with a master's degree. Wow! I did it!

I no longer qualified for the homeless veteran program, so Maria wanted me to move back home. I had a great job now—a dream job in a big office with my master's degree hanging in *my* office on the wall behind my big desk. So cool! And I had the *highest salary* I had ever had in my life!

My daughter, Myra, had grown up now. My wife, Maria, was a great cook, and I enjoyed eating at home the best (if you know what I mean)!

I knew that was where I belonged, with my loving, beautiful wife, Maria, and helping others with recovery. Myra was over twenty-one years old now, and she was "lukewarm" friendly to me because she had *never completely forgiven me for my past drunken behavior.* I attended twelve-step meetings. Life was *good*, for a while.

My employment was *close to home*, and I was also sought out as a "main speaker" at twelve-step meetings. I was able to help lots of people, especially homeless people and street ladies to *get off the streets* and into recovery programs. It was called "doing twelve-step work."

The last time that I had checked up on my Pavement Princess, Brenda, I told her that I was *proud of her*. She was *still clean (off drugs) and sober*, doing okay, going to her meetings, and living with another senior citizen, who was moderately wealthy and took care of her.

But that was a year ago. Little did I realize that Brenda had relapsed since then. She started using drugs again *two months ago*. This time, her "disease" of heroin addiction *took big bites* out of her. It was killing her slowly, even quicker now.

Out of the blue, I got a surprise phone call from *Natasha*!

"Hi, Stuart," she said. "Remember me? It's *Natasha*! Hey, I bet Brenda didn't tell you, but I'm in the twelve-step program too now! *I have over six years of sobriety*!"

"Wow!" I exclaimed. "Natasha? You? Six years of sobriety? That's great! I was wondering what became of you. Maybe I'll see you at a twelve-step meeting sometime, or we can go to one together!"

"Yeah, I want to *thank you*, Stuart! When Brenda told me that you went to rehab and got sober, *I couldn't believe it*! Then I learned that it was *you who took Brenda* to rehab and *she got clean from heroin! That was the most incredible thing I ever saw!* I never thought that I'd *ever* see Brenda *off drugs*! So I thought, well, if Stuart and Brenda can get clean and sober using the twelve-step program, just maybe, *so can I*! So I signed up for rehab six years ago, and I have been *sober ever since*."

"That is such great news, Natasha," I said. "But what about Brenda?"

"Until a couple of months ago, Brenda was going to Narcotics Anonymous twelve-step meetings with me," Natasha continued. "Well...sometimes. But then, *she stopped going to meetings altogether.* And when I went last week to see how she was doing, I saw that *she was a mess!* She looked fat, had her teeth knocked out in a fight."

"Oh no!" I sadly said.

"And I've got *even worse news for you,* Stuart," she reluctantly added.

"Okay, what?" I gasped, fearing the worst.

"*Brenda is in the hospital!*" Natasha said. "Brenda's mother called me, trying to find you, and said, 'Brenda goes in and out of a coma and is delirious!' Brenda's mother says that Brenda keeps asking, 'Where is my road dog, Stuart?' That's why I'm calling you," she explained.

I was stunned and didn't know what to say.

"Stuart, you need to go see Brenda *now!*" Natasha warned. "That is...if you want to see *her alive again!*"

"But Natasha," I pleaded, "I'm spending Thanksgiving with my family and relatives right now. Can't it *wait* until *tomorrow?*"

"No!" Natasha cried out. "Stuart, if ever she needed you the most, it's today! You need to get to the hospital *right now!*"

"Thanks for telling me, Natasha," I said. "I'm on my way."

I hung up the phone, still in shock over the news.

"Who was that?" Maria asked.

"Maria, I just got word that an old friend of mine is seriously ill and in the hospital. Someone in the twelve-step program has *relapsed.* You know how *that goes,* Maria. I *have to go see them.* I love you, Maria! Hey! Save me some turkey dinner. I'll be right back as soon as I can."

Luckily, the hospital where Brenda was being cared for was only one mile away from my house. I got there in ten minutes and parked my car.

I went to the hospital gift shop and bought her a teddy bear and a bunch of flowers and asked the hospital receptionist where I could find Brenda.

"Oh, Brenda's in *intensive care,*" the receptionist said. "She's in very serious condition. Are you a relative?"

"Yes, I am," I answered. "I am her road dog," I mumbled.

"Her what?" the receptionist questioned, shaking her head. "Okay...you can go up."

When I got to Brenda's hospital bed, she was surrounded by about ten people, who all said they were all Brenda's relatives. The guy that she had been living with was not invited to see her because they *thought* it was him who

273

bought her the drugs. But I knew it wasn't that guy's fault. It was Roscoe doing it *again*! It was common knowledge in twelve-step programs. If you were a real hardcore alcoholic or addict and you stopped going to meetings as a life-style, there was a *big chance you will relapse and die*! It was a *serious business*. Going to twelve-step meetings could mean a difference between life and death. So far, I'd been going to twelve-step meetings like clockwork, and calling up my sponsor, Jo C., twice a week.

Lying in the hospital bed, Brenda looked like she was *sleeping peacefully*.

"Hey Brenda!" I called out. "This is *your road dog*, Stuart! I just now heard and came to see you!"

I kissed her and held her hand. "Hey, *wake up*!" I shouted.

There was a heartbeat monitor beeping over her head. A voice behind me said, "She has been that way for *two weeks* now." It was Brenda's mom. "Thanks for coming, Stuart," she said.

Just then, a Catholic priest came in and prayed over Brenda for a few minutes. Brenda was Catholic. The priest had given her her "last rites."

I told Brenda, "Brenda, it's *okay*. I'm here. *You are tired*. Remember, *I'll always love you*. It's a miracle we both made it alive to the *year*

2000! We never thought we would! If you can hear me, Brenda, please *blink your eyes.*"

Suddenly, she blinked!

"*I'm* proud of you, Brenda!" I said. "You *stayed clean!*"

Then a smile came across her face. And then the monitor *flatlined* while I was holding her hand.

The nurse said, "*She's gone!*"

Brenda died that day. My Higher Power let me be there at this precise moment. *Why?*

Her mom said to me, "Stuart, I think Brenda was waiting for you to come before she let go."

I went back home to Maria and my family. I felt like relapsing now myself. I was sad and heartbroken over Brenda's death. Natasha phoned me and said, "Hey, Stuart, more news! Roscoe was found in Brenda's room, naked, and *dead from a heroin overdose*, with a needle still in his arm!"

But now, instead of needing a drink, I knew the substitute for alcohol was to go to a twelve-step meeting. I also told my sponsor, Jo C., and he told me, "Everyone who is family or a friend is a gift from God on loan to you. It was just her time, Stuart. And Brenda *got her revenge* on Roscoe!"

I told Maria that a fellow alcoholic addict had just died because she stopped going to meetings and relapsed.

"That's too bad, Stuart," Maria said, comforting me.

"Yes, Maria, there was nothing I could do about it," I answered. *But I knew that Maria knew it was Brenda!*

"Someday, Maria, I want to open a recovery home, or sober living place, so I can help others like my friend who died, as well as others, just so they could have a place to go to *stay* clean and sober. I envision a place run by alcoholics for alcoholics and other addicts too, of course—a sober living home based on the twelve steps," I said to my wife.

"Well, Stuart," Maria said, "whatever *you* need to do to stay sober, I will help you any way I can. I like you much better *sober* than drunk. Stuart, if marrying me and having a family was the first thing you did right, then the second thing you're doing right is *staying sober!*"

"Yes, Maria, *I've been through a lot* in recovery, and I have accomplished things I'd never been able to do had I not stopped drinking. I myself, because of my meetings and spiritual program, am a miracle! But what's *next*? I need another mountain to climb."

I planned to get my doctorate degree next. So I sent away to various colleges for information on PhD programs. Then one day, I went to the Veteran's Hospital for a checkup, and a doctor there told me that I was restored to *good health* because I stopped drinking. But he added, "Stuart, you need *more exercise*."

"What should I do, Doctor?" I asked.

"Stuart," he said, "I'm a runner. I run the Los Angeles Marathon every year. Lots of nurses and doctors run it because, right in town, there is a runner's club called The Leapers who meet outside the hospital every Sunday morning at 6:00 a.m. to train for the next Los Angeles Marathon. Why don't *you* join us, Stuart?"

"That's crazy!" I exclaimed. "Me? Run 26.2 miles in the Los Angeles Marathon?"

"It will keep you healthy," the doctor said.

I liked that idea, and right then and there, I made up my mind to run it. I showed up early next Sunday and joined The Leapers running club. They gave me a bright-pink T-shirt to wear because we run on country roads and didn't want cars to hit us. So every Sunday morning, I was running down country roads in a pink T-shirt, training to run in the next LA Marathon!

Maria and my family were proud of me for completing my education.

I told my friends and family next, "Guess what, Maria?"

"What?" Maria asked.

"Your husband Stuart is going to run in the next Los Angeles Marathon," I told her.

Maria looked surprised. "You?" she asked. "Are you *sure you can do it*?"

"No," I admitted, "but my goal is not how fast I run. I just want to find out if *I have the endurance to do it*! If I don't finish the 26.2 miles, I'll *die* trying. You know, Maria, that in the very first marathon, the first runner died at the end in Greece."

Maria said, "I love you. I believe in you. And I know *you can do anything you set out to do, Stuart!*"

So the day came when I ran in the 2002 Los Angeles Marathon. My whole family cheered me on. My sister and her husband even came to watch me. My whole family cheered me on. I ran 26.2 miles that day *because I was sober!*

And I was awarded a finisher medal on a ribbon around my neck. I finished in six hours and thirty-three minutes. Then, my family and I went to dinner in a fancy restaurant. *These were good days.* Indeed, I got my family back.

During the next year, my daughter, Myra, joined The Leapers running club too. Myra even brought some of her friends to train for the 2003 Los Angeles Marathon.

I felt happy. I was part of my family again, but I had not realized that I was *skipping my twelve-step meetings.* I was slowly becoming a dry drunk without even realizing it—DRY=doing recovery yourself.

My long-term sponsor Jo C. moved out of California to somewhere back east. He was gone and was not coming back. So now, *I was without a twelve-step sponsor. Not good!*

I did get a new cat named Smokey. When I was sober, cats *liked* me. Everyone did because I was a *good guy* then.

It was the 2003 marathon day. I ran it, and my daughter, Myra, joined me. Maria, my sister, and her husband cheered us on.

Myra ran along near me for the beginning of the LA Marathon, and Myra just had fun and came in later at about seven hours for 26.2 miles.

After the second Los Angeles Marathon, I was *really* becoming a dry drunk—no sponsor, slacking off on my twelve-step meetings. My employment was going well, but I was getting bored. And I filled out paperwork to get a promotion to supervisor. I still wanted to go higher and to get more out of life.

After the second LA Marathon, I thought things were good with my family, but not going to meetings became getting closer to that first drink again.

The twelve-step program was going on the back burner by me not going to meetings, and the holidays were here again. It was Christmas time again, and at my office, someone gave me alcohol *as a gift*—a bottle of Captain Morgan's spiced rum. And the bottle seemed to be *talking to me*, saying, *"Drink me, Stuart! No one will know!"*

I had had a rough day isolating. I began feeling sorry for myself. I was consumed with "poor me" thoughts. Time to pour me a drink. So I decided *maybe* I could *just* take *one drink!* I stopped at a convenience store and got a cup of ginger ale and poured the rum in it. I was lying to myself in my own voice in my head. At first, my voice told me, "You can have *one drink*. You *can't really* be an alcoholic, Stuart. You've been sober for thirteen years. *You are cured now!*"

As I raised the glass of alcohol to my lips, I was just about to take that *first drink* again. Suddenly, there *was another voice in my head. It was the voice of my sponsor, Jo C.* Even though he wasn't my sponsor anymore, I heard *his voice* in my mind telling me, *"Wait. Stop! Stuart, play the drinking tape all the way through before you take that first drink!"*

And then, in my mind's eye, I remembered *all the voices* of people in twelve-step meetings and what I had heard and learned in there for all these years. So *just in time*, before I *almost relapsed* to drinking alcohol, voices in my head said these things to me:

> Stuart, you don't have to take another drink for the rest of your life if you don't want to! Stuart, *get your ass to a meeting! Now!* Stuart, stay away from the *first*

drink! Stuart! Don't be stuck on stupid.

And then it hit me. I realized *it was the first drink that got you drunk.* Then you SLIP when sobriety *lost its* priority!

The voice in my head continued to warn me, "Stay sober until midnight. It's one day at a time. Stuart, *your job really is to stay sober!* Stuart, ask for help from your Higher Power! Stuart, for you to drink again is to *die!*"

I recognized that all of those twelve-step meetings had *ruined* my enjoyment of drinking.

"Okay, God," I said, "*I heard you!*"

And I poured out my *deadly drink*, put down the glass, went back to twelve-step meetings—three times per day—and went back to ninety meetings in ninety days.

I knew that I could no longer *ever enjoy drinking alcohol* or taking other drugs, knowing and remembering the physical, emotional, and spiritual damage it caused me and others. And I knew for sure that a *headful* of recovery and a *bellyful* of booze just didn't mix!

I knew what I needed to do now. I needed to open a sober living home and help others to maintain sobriety.

CHAPTER TWENTY-FOUR

The Club
Dreams of Sober Living

MEETING ROOM

After working all day in a large office where I was a professional counselor helping others, I knew I needed a meeting.

I had learned in meetings that my number one priority was to get to a recovery meeting.

282

My job was a gift, resulting from staying with my recovery program. In other words, without meetings, I would not have a job or anything else. My wife and I were happy now, and family life was on the mend.

I was sober now for thirteen years. But I remembered I used to drink every day for thirty years, so as a replacement for that behavior, I found that a meeting every day kept me sane and sober. So even with all those years of sobriety under my belt, I still went to meetings every day.

There were twelve-step clubs all over the country and world that had twelve-step meetings every day. Some, five or six meetings per day. So today, I would try another club that I had not been to before. It was called Alano Club, and it was located near the mountains in a small town (Alano = *Alcoholics Anonymous*).

Since I'd never been there before, at another Alano Club, I had a good sober friend named Dave, a handsome guy with twenty years' sobriety who offered to take me there. He looked like movie star—sort of a cross between Clint Eastwood and Jack Palance. Dave had a dual diagnosis but stayed sober and went to meetings every day. Some people said he was not too bright. But I knew him, and he was a really cool guy. Even though he had more sobriety time than I did, he was attracted to my recovery program and asked me to be his sponsor. So we went around to speaker meetings where I was a main speaker, and he was my ten minute speaker. When Dave was not at meetings, he worked as a roofer.

On this day, he showed me where the hidden Alano Club was. This club was set up like a bar but served coffee. It had two separate twelve-step meeting rooms in the back, and in front of the bar structure were barstools. This room was called the Half Measures Room because there were tables and chairs in there, and recovering people could relax there between meetings.

The lady behind the bar-like counter who worked there was a volunteer worker who did not get paid. She was an old friend of Dave's, and he introduced me to her. Her name was Mary. A funny thing I noticed about Mary was that all she wanted to talk about—every word that came out of her mouth—was about twelve-step programs and recovery. So we really hit it off. We seemed to be two of a kind. She was a very nice lady. We became instant "sobriety" friends.

It happened to be Tuesday evening at the club, and Mary told us tonight was Taco Tuesday—two tacos for a dollar. So I bought tacos for Dave, Mary, and myself.

We all sat at the cafe-style table, and we talked. I told them, "Well, there are a lot of people in recovery who need a safe place to live where there is no drinking or drugging going on."

"Yes," Mary agreed, "we need to change playgrounds and playmates in recovery and find new friends who think like we do who are not drinking and using."

So for a while after I continued going to that Alano Club every Tuesday evening for Taco Tuesday and to chat about recovery with Mary, I then told her about an idea I had. I told her that someday I wanted to start my own sober living home. "I have thirteen years of sobriety now, and I need to get more involved in twelve-step programs by helping others because I'd been sober this long. Yes, Mary, I even have a good job today and my own large office and a secretary." I handed Mary my business card.

Mary said to me, "Wow, I've never known many people in here who even have a job, let alone a college education!"

I told her, "Mary, it's all a gift from staying sober one day at a time for thirteen years. Mary, I was a high school dropout before I got sober at age forty-seven. I graduated college with a master's degree at age fifty-five."

"Tell me more," said Mary.

My beautiful and wonderful wife, Maria, and I made arrangements to refinance our home and put it in my wife's name and for me to have the equity money to help buy and set up my sober living home.

At another meeting on a Friday night, I shared about my idea, and then I met Suzie, who has just gotten her real estate license. She told me, "Hey, we can help each other. I need to make a sale in my new job, and you need to buy some property." So soon she called me up. "I found your place," she said.

My wife and I drove up to look at it. It looked good from the street. It was a fixer-upper: two houses, one main house, and a duplex on two and a half acres. But the owner yelled at us and chased us away because we did not have an appointment. But I knew in my heart I was destined to own that property.

My sober real estate agent friend Suzie called me. "Sorry, the property you want has been sold to someone else. I can show you some more places." I looked at several more places, but still my thoughts were only on that first place. People told me, "Why would you want that place? It's run-down and between the freeway and some railroad tracks, and it's in the middle of nowhere." My thoughts were *this would be perfect for a sober living home because it is not in a bad neighborhood because there is no neighborhood!* The place was in escrow with another buyer.

So each Tuesday Taco night, I was telling my story to Mary and going to a meeting at the club. Then, one day it happened. Suzie called me up and told me that the place I wanted was on the market again and she had made an appointment for my wife and I to see it.

When my wife and I saw it, it was a mess—everything in each part of it was broken and ugly. But in my mind's eye, I had a vision of what the place would be like and look like. It would have a twelve-step meeting room and beds for recovering alcoholics. I'd make it the best sober living home in California! So I bought the property, and we began fixing it up. It would be called Sobriety Castle.

Back at the club, I told Mary, "Yes, I now have the property and a meeting room. I need to start a meeting there on a Friday night, but I will need a meeting secretary."

Mary said, "I will do it."

"Yes, Mary," I replied, "but it's an hour drive for you, and usually a secretary commitment is for a year." The reason I chose Mary was because she would be perfect because she lived and breathed twelve-step programs.

And Mary said to me, "Yes, I will do it for a year," and the first twelve-step meeting on a Friday night at Sobriety Castle was planned out.

So in the first week of January, the property belonged to me. A screened porch was selected to become the twelve-step meeting room.

I returned to the club on Tuesday and told Mary that I now owned the place that would later become a sober living home. We were ready for a meeting. So the first Friday night in April, I picked up Mary at the club, and we headed for an hour's ride through the mountains. We did not want to be late for our first meeting at my new place. We got stuck in a traffic jam. Mary and I envisioned lots of people attending our first meeting there. Mary was now the secretary of the meeting and was ready! I called my wife, Maria, who was there, helping to clean and fix up the houses. "Anyone there yet?" I asked.

She replied, "Oh yes, lots of people."

Mary and I were concerned because we were still stuck in traffic and would be twenty minutes late. So finally, my car entered my property to an empty driveway except for one car in front.

So we had our first twelve-step meeting on that first Friday night of the year. In attendance was Mary, myself, and our sober real estate agent friend Suzie.

When the twelve-step meeting was over, Suzie drove Mary home. *We shut all the lights off.*

My wife, Maria, and I strolled out, hand-in-hand, onto our big dark front yard. Maria said to me, "Hey, Stuart, I've been *noticing* something strange. There is something funny going on next door at our new neighbors."

"What makes you think that?" I said.

"All those cars," she said. "And why do they have a *red porch light*?"

There were two neighboring houses. On the right was the people who sold me the house. On the left was the house with the red porch light on last night. Now I had been afraid of what the neighbors would think because I was about to open up my sober living houses.

When I found out that the house on my left was a *swinger's club*, I was *relieved*. Wow, I guess if the neighborhood was okay with that swinger's club, they would have no problem with my sober living home plans!

Even though I had a live-and-let-live attitude about the swinger's club next door, that was not so with my wife, Maria, who stared down the residents, giving them the evil eye, which she had often given me before I got sober!

After that, they packed up, closed it down, and moved. It was for the best. I did not need any more temptations nor did my future array of sober living residents.

CHAPTER TWENTY-FIVE

Ren Fair Joan and Creating Sobriety Castle

The future Sobriety Castle property was a disaster when I bought it even though it had three houses on it. The meeting room was created out of a screened porch in the first house. The other two houses had been rented out before I came, and *those houses* were in *total shambles*.

During the week, I worked hard trying to fix up all three houses as fast as I could—new plumbing, new paint, electrical repair, carpeting, new appliances, *everything*! I rented an airless paint sprayer. I used to be a painter and dreaded being up on a ladder again. But soon, all three sober living houses were *painted* to look like *brand-new* inside and out in a short time. I realized that I could even paint faster and better while sober!

The front house was to be where I would reside during the week, going to see my wife, Maria, every weekend. The middle house would become "Ladies Gone Sober"—a sober living home for ladies. The end house would be for men and was called "The Sober Guys"—a sober living home. The whole property would be called "Sobriety Castle."

While fixing up my property, I'd always had help from my Higher Power, who always put what I needed in front of me when I needed it!

The first thing I needed was information on *how* to run a sober living home. I saw an ad in the *Los Angeles Times*. Somebody ran an ad on how to start and run a sober living home by the California's Sober Living Association Club. So I took the course and also signed on to belong to their club as the public relations manager of it.

The definition of a sober living home was a home where *all the residents* had a *similar malady or disability* and simply had a right to *choose to live together as a family*. And the *disability* for sober living qualification was the disease of alcoholism or other drug addictions, in other words, *chemical dependency*.

So *before* I opened the doors of my sober living home, *I got educated about it* and learned and followed *a code of ethics and guidelines to operate it correctly*. Yes, I'd create the *best* sober living home in California!

Across the street was a large field, and then there was a large county park. From my property, I could hear the commotion from the park. My daughter, Myra, and I went to check it out. In the park this month was a medieval-period Renaissance fair going on—a yearly event. How cool! The participants were setting it up on this day, and we just walked in and saw *rehearsals* going on.

This day Sobriety Castle was destined to set its first paying unlikely tenant. Around noon, a fancy car pulled in Stuart's driveway. Suddenly a beautiful lady from the Ren fair squeezed out her car. She was all deck out in her elegant, royal medieval costume booby dress with an eight-foot-wide hoop dress!

"I can't believe my eyes!" Stuart said. "Am I dreaming?"

The lady spoke excitedly, "Please help me. I work at the Ren fair across the street." She begged, "Please let me stay in a room at your place. I can pay you $800 per week if I can stay here or whatever you want, but that's what I pay now at the hotel."

"Come inside, and let's talk," I said invitingly.

I explained to Ren fair Joan that *she* would be the very *first resident* I ever had and also told her, "It's a *sober living home*! Here, *we don't drink or use drugs*." And I showed her the twelve-step meeting room and explained that all twelve-step meetings were free and were being held here *every* night and that she and her Ren fair associates were welcome at any time to attend meetings.

Ren fair Joan had some trouble sitting down on my sofa with her big hoop dress.

Nevertheless, she said, "Stuart, this place is absolutely perfect! I'll take it!"

I showed her the back house. That was the only house that was reasonably habitable at this point as renovations were almost complete.

"One thing more, Joan," I added, "I stay there too, so you won't have to be all alone. And I'll have to ask my wife, Maria, to verify that you can stay."

Ren fair Joan said, "*I really love the place, Stuart. I need to relax and practice. And what a big private backyard you have behind this house too!*"

"Well, it can be seen from the freeway cars, Joan," I explained. "But that's all."

Going by the residence was a public highway with about five hundred thousand cars a week passing by there.

I called Maria. She said, "Stuart, *we need the money. If you* think *that lady is okay*, then let her stay. I'll buy new beddings, curtains, and new mattresses. You come and pick them up at the store."

I hung up the phone.

"Okay," I told Joan. "You can move in tomorrow. We will have it all *nice* for you."

"Did you say $800 per week?" I asked to verify the amount again.

"Sure, I did," she answered. "Stuart, here it is in an advanced payment," she replied, handing me eight one hundred-dollar bills. "Oh... *one* more thing, though, Stuart."

"What's that?" I asked.

"I have two dogs and a cat. They always travel with me. So here is $200 more to allow my three pets to stay too."

"Anything else, Ren fair Joan?" I asked, sensing that there was more to her requests.

"Actually, yes!" she admitted. "I will want to bring a fellow performer in the afternoon to practice in your backyard. His name is Stanley."

"Of course," I said, wanting to be as accommodating as possible to my first new tenant.

Ren fair Joan moved in. She had about at least ten costumes and one suit of chain mail armor. She was very pretty and sexy and wore the low-cut Ren fair "booby" dresses well— both as royalty or as a peasant. She explained more about herself to me that while some people ran away to join a circus, Joan ran away to join a *traveling* Renaissance fair, which traveled all over the United States.

She *loved it* and followed the fair everywhere. However, Joan would be staying here for *only* a few weeks, and then she would be moving on.

Ren fair Joan also admitted, "Yes." She drank alcohol, but she said that she was *not an alcoholic*, although she knew some of her friends who were Ren fair performers who were in twelve-step programs and were looking for a local meeting to go to.

"And, Stuart, one *more* thing," she added. "I can get *you and your family* and *anyone who lives here free tickets to get into the Ren fair*!"

"Now you're talking, Ren fair Joan!" I said.

I told my wife, Maria, and my daughter, Myra, "Hey, guess what, my Myra! We have tickets for next weekend to go to the Ren fair! And not only that, I've got a performer who will show us *an inside tour of the show*. Her name is Ren fair Joan."

"That sounds cool, Dad," Myra said.

"Can we buy costumes?"

"Yes, certainly!" I assured her. "We will get dressed up as in Old England."

"Very cool, Dad!" she exclaimed.

Ren fair Joan moved in that night from the downtown hotel to a room next to mine. I installed a new lock on her door so she'd feel safe. The backyard of that duplex was *big* and *fenced in*, perfect for her two dogs. Her cat *stayed inside* because of the coyotes roaming around the neighborhood.

Ren fair Joan said that she also rode horses in "the show."

After she settled in, I went to my room and took a nap. It was evening, and it was beginning to get dark. *All of a sudden*, in my backyard, I saw a *bright fire*!

Somebody had Joan *tied up to a pole with wood around it, and a fire was raging!* I heard fire engine trucks driving on my driveway. They ran to the backyard and screamed.

"What's going on in here?" the lead fireman asked.

"I don't know!" I said, somewhat astonished.

In the backyard, Ren fair Joan was getting sprayed with water as was her friend. She said, "Hey, I thought *you* said I *could rehearse for my show,* Stuart!"

"What do you mean?" I asked. She was dressed in chain mail armor now.

"I play *Joan of Arc* at the show," she said. "It's a *controlled* fire. We do it all the time. It's okay, Stuart. Stanley here is *my assistant.*"

So Ren fair Joan signed some *papers with the firemen,* and she also volunteered to pay for the firemen's trip out to the property. During the rest of the night, I got a free "preview show" out my back window as Ren fair Joan and Stanley did tightrope walking acts and juggled sticks on fire. It was great. They were both extremely talented!

My daughter, Myra, and I were *all excited.* This Saturday morning, we were going to the Ren fair with our *free tickets.* It also happened to be Myra's birthday.

Going through a medieval entrance gate, we were now inside the very large Ren fair village with paths leading in all directions.

There were paths leading everywhere, cheerful sounds of medieval music, endless colorful street performers dressed as nobility or peasants, all speaking in the language of Old English from the sixteenth century. It was as if we went back in time! Such fun!

Since Ren fair Joan had promised us a *private* tour, we began to search for her. The fair was huge, going for miles. It even had a live jousting tournament, with knights in armor on horses.

Finally, we found Stanley's show. He was on a tightrope, on a unicycle, juggling knives, and telling jokes to the audience, who were sitting on logs. When he took a break, we said, "Hi, Stanley! We made it! *Good show!* We enjoyed it! Hey, where might we find Ren fair Joan?"

"She's over in the next booth area," Stanley replied. "She's been expecting you!"

I was dressed in a homemade silly-looking Ren fair costume, and Ren fair Joan made fun of my lack of knowledge of the Renaissance period costumes. I introduced my daughter, Myra.

I informed Joan that *today* was *Myra's birthday* and we were *celebrating it* by coming to the fair. Myra's homemade Ren fair outfit looked barely passable to Ren fair Joan. She said, "Come with me, Stuart. *You* need to buy yourself a new hat. Your two-dollar Robin Hood hat *won't work here*! You look ridiculous!"

Already, Myra was telling me, "Dad, Ren fair Joan is *too bossy! I don't like her!*"

We went into a huge Ren fair costume store with thousands of very nice costumes for sale but all *very expensive.* Myra started admiring a beautiful noble lady's dress. We looked at the price—$295. Wow!

"These are so expensive!" Myra declared.

"Put it down. You can't afford it!" Joanie *snapped* at Myra. "Now, Stuart, *I'll* help you pick out a new hat *for yourself!*"

Now, even *I* thought that Joan was acting mean toward Myra, and I wondered why because I thought Ren fair Joan was nice.

"Stuart, I'll show you three hats," she began. "Then you choose one of them, okay?" So up on the shelf were hundreds of Ren fair hats of all types. "Your Robin Hood hat has to go!"

"Try this hat on first," Ren fair Joan commanded as she handed me a light-blue ladies' princess cone hat with a veil hanging from the end. I put it on. I thought it was funny, but Myra was *not* amused.

Okay, second hat. Joan handed me a very nice green and gold court jester's hat. Again, I thought it was funny, but Myra was not pleased at all.

Finally, the third hat was a cavalier-type hat, which was the hat that Ren fair Joan wanted me to buy after all. And it was perfect with a large ostrich feather in it. I looked pretty good now and in style for the Ren fair.

Ren fair Joan said, "Listen, I have to go back to work. You can walk around with Myra. Come back later."

"Okay, sounds good," I said.

"I don't like her, Dad," Myra said, complaining. "She is mean!"

"Myra, it's your birthday. At least I can buy you a T-shirt or something," I said, consoling my daughter. "Maybe Ren fair Joan is just having a bad day or something."

So Myra and I had a wonderful time by ourselves, enjoying all the sights and games at the Ren fair. A *giant wooden swing* and the jousting tournament were both fantastic! But it was time to go home now.

"Let's find Ren fair Joan so we can get out of here," Myra suggested.

"Let me find her first. I'll meet you there. You stay here."

When I get to Ren fair Joan's show area, I was astonished to find Ren fair Joan and my daughter, Myra *both drunk!*

"What's going on, Myra?" I asked in utter amazement. "Do you drink alcohol?"

"Dad, I'm an alcoholic and a drug addict too, just like you!" she admitted. "Didn't you know?"

"Come on, Myra," I said. "We will talk about this later. And *shame on you*, Ren fair Joan!"

"It's not *my* fault, Stuart," Joan answered snappily. "It was Myra's idea to drink a beer! Anyway, Myra, *this is for you. Happy birthday!*"

Myra took a large gift-wrapped box from Ren fair Joan and went home to my property. I wondered what the present was.

"What is it?" I asked Myra. "What did Ren fair Joan give you for your birthday?"

When we opened it, we were all surprised.

It was the $295 dress Myra had admired. That was nice of Ren fair Joan.

CHAPTER TWENTY-SIX

Meetings at the Castle

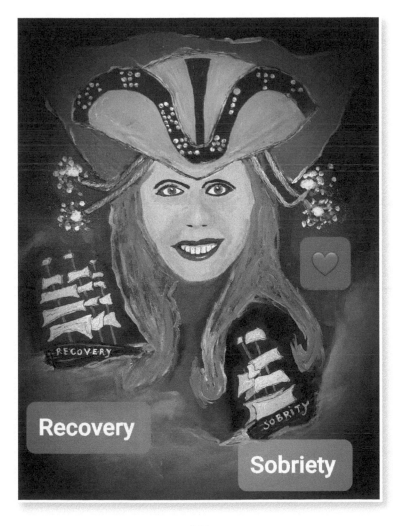

Mary's Friday night twelve-step meeting was going well now, and also, there were meetings every night of the week. Saturday was a speaker's meeting. Sundays were a candlelight meeting.

There was a lighted sign that could be seen from the highway, indicating that there were twelve-step meetings, so the meeting attendance was good now—anywhere from five to thirty people at a given time visiting our meeting room.

Dolores, a.k.a. "Doris the Doll Face," was *sober* again and got a job on cable TV as a host on a home shopping channel. She drives a Bentley Arnage automobile. She was the secretary of the Saturday night speaker's twelve-step meeting. And Natasha went back to junior college and was now a drug and alcohol counselor at Cedarwood Recovery Center's Women's Program. On Saturday night, Natasha brought a van full of ladies to attend the twelve-step speaker meeting.

This Saturday, the main speaker was someone with fifty-five years of sobriety named Ridley. He was ninety years old. I had not heard him speak before.

I was upset with Myra and Ren fair Joan for drinking, but I kept my cool about it. Who knew? Maybe they were *not* real alcoholics like I was. I calmly talk to Ren fair Joan and said, "I know *you say you don't* have a drinking problem, but maybe, *just for fun* and in the spirit of doing something different, *you* can check out our twelve-step meeting. You can invite some of your friends from the Renaissance fair to *this Saturday night's* twelve-step speaker meeting. It's free. Meetings are *always free* and include free coffee and free cookies! After Saturday's Ren fair, *come over!* It starts at 7:30 p.m. Aren't you curious what it's about?"

"Sure, Stuart," Joan replied. "It *might* be *interesting*. I've *never been to a twelve-step meeting before*."

I called my wife, Maria, and explained all that was going on. Maria said, "I want to come too, and I'll try to bring Myra."

"Good," I answered, "I hope Myra and Ren fair Joan will hear something." Usually, the meetings were a "weird" form of entertainment at worst.

I also phoned my AA friend, Mary, and said, "Hey, Mary, I know you're coming Friday to run a meeting, but we need you to be our ten-minute speaker. Our Saturday night secretary, Dolores, asked me to ask you."

"Okay," said Mary, "you know I never said no to a twelve-step request. I'll be there!"

It looked like it would be a very interesting twelve-step meeting coming up this Saturday. The remaining mystery was that none of us had heard the main speaker before and nobody knew him.

Saturday night was here. Cars were coming into the driveway and were parking. My years-long AA college friend, Bill, rode in on his motorcycle. He had just graduated with a PhD in social work from Berkeley, California. He unlocked the meeting room door and put on the large coffeepot. It was percolating!

Dolores drove in the driveway in her Bentley Arnage with loud music playing. The song was "Back to Black" by Amy Winehouse. She carried a tray of cookies to the meeting room. Dolores said, "I almost hit some bum on a bike!"

A van arrived with ladies. Natasha brought them from Cedarwood Recovery Center. Another van arrived with men from there also.

Coming in the driveway were eight weird-looking people *on foot, walking*! All were dressed up in *crazy* costumes. It was the *Ren fair people*! They came!

So it was the largest meeting yet—and one of the strangest.

There was one parking place in front of the meeting room saved for the *main speaker*. Where the heck was he?

A car drove in. It was my wife, Maria, and Myra. Good! Another car—it was Mary!

As the meeting progressed, the introductions and twelve-step readings were quickly done, and Mary finished her *excellent* ten-minute talk. There was a fifteen-minute break.

Everyone wondered, *Where is our main speaker?*

Everyone was drinking coffee, eating cookies, engaged in friendly chatter, waiting for *tonight's big event—the main speaker!*

As we looked to the dark driveway entrance, we saw somebody coming in *on a bicycle!* He parked in the reserved parking place.

"Hi, I'm *Ridley*, your *main speaker* for tonight! Sorry I'm a little late. *Some* crazy driver almost ran over me!"

We all welcomed tonight's main speaker, Ridley, and after *he* had some cookies and coffee, the meeting resumed. Dolores said, "Tonight's *main speaker is Ridley with fifty-five years sober!*"

Very soon Ridley had us all *spellbound* with his many drunk and sobriety stories. The first thing he told us is "I'm ninety years old with fifty-five years of continuous *sobriety*, and I've been attending twelve-step meetings for over fifty-five years. Why? *Because it works!* Bottom line was, I'm not here *because* I'm old. I'm old *because* I'm here! And countless *miracles* have happened in my life!"

Ridley did *not* look ninety years old but more like *sixty*. Ridley continued, "In recovery, if you *don't* drink, a day at a time, you get *better looking, smarter, healthier, and happier each day!* I was *ugly* when I came in. Now, I'm *handsome!* I had *no* self-esteem, but now I have

305

high self-esteem! For me to take a drink again *is to die*! So I don't drink, and I don't die! That's how *you* get to be a long-timer in AA. Simply, *don't* drink and *don't* die! Twelve-step programs are *not* for those that *need* it but rather for those that *want* it and *do* it. *It is a way of life*. Sometimes you stay sober for a minute at a time, sometimes a day at a time. And the days turn into weeks. The weeks turn into months, and the months turn into years. For me, it's *fifty-five years* of continuous sobriety! And I live *in today*! *These* are the good old days, *right now*! *Life is in session*. Are *you here right now*, or are you living in the past? Or *are you* living in the *future*? I live in *the now*, enjoying each moment. And no matter where you are in your recovery, the *best* days of your existence lie ahead of you all. Work all the twelve steps, read the book, and, above all, get yourself a Higher Power!

"And *this meeting is great*! All you *Ren fair* actors and actresses sure make this an even more interesting meeting! I heard Queen Anne over there [referring to *another* lady in costume] just got her *first* thirty-day sobriety chip *tonight*. I remember how difficult that was for me many, many years ago. *Those first thirty days*, one day at a time, *seemed endless*. *It was hard*. Let me tell you, queen. My fifty-five years of sobriety went by quicker than your first thirty days. I'm proud of you tonight. By the way, get rid of your king husband before you lose your head!"

Stuart was amazed to see sitting there quietly there back in the corner of the meeting room were the "real" *Ghost of Queen Anne and Black Beard* listening intently and enjoying his twelve-step meeting this night. Stuart was happy only he could see them.

Just by attending only one twelve-step meeting, both ghosts let go of their checkered past and became happy, joyous, and free thereafter.

We all had a good laugh and learned a lot at that meeting. Ren fair Joan said, "You were right, Stuart. That was an interesting experience! The Ren fair is leaving town tomorrow, but wherever I go and travel, I'll try to check out a twelve-step meeting thanks to you."

Myra and Maria came up to me. I kissed my wife. "That was a good message," said Maria.

Myra said, "Yeah, it was okay...but *I'm not ready to stop drinking yet, Dad.* I'm not *that* bad!"

The Saturday night speaker's meeting was over. People were getting in their cars to drive home or go out for coffee at a Denny's. Others were still standing in front of the meeting room, chatting in the evening darkness.

The Ren fair people walked back to their camp. It was a perfect evening. Only *one person* remained: *our speaker* Ridley with his bike.

"Are you going to ride your bike home?" I asked, concerned about the late hour and his age.

"Heck no!" he answered. "*My wife* is picking me up in our van."

Just then, a van pulled up. A pretty lady hopped out and kissed Ridley. "This is *my wife, Sherry.* She has twenty-four years of sobriety."

"She doesn't even look twenty-four!" I said.

Bottom line was, *Ridley was right!* Drinking and using *aged* you faster, while sobriety and recovery made you look and feel *younger!*

After a perfect evening, it got even better: to go home with my wife Maria, and my daughter Myra. Home was happy and peaceful. I was thinking, *Ridley is right again! Sobriety keeps getting better and better!*

As I held my beautiful loving wife Maria, in my arms, we were watching TV—Maria and I on the sofa and Myra on the easy chair, *It doesn't get any better than this! Life is good!* I was thinking.

CHAPTER TWENTY-SEVEN

Building a Good Reputation

Sobriety Castle Sober Living Home was about to open up for residents. Since I once owned an advertising agency, I knew how to create nice-looking *advertising* flyers and also how to write press releases.

Since sober living was not for everyone, I posted flyers up on bulletin boards in as many twelve-step Alano clubs as I could and on bulletin boards in all of the "recovery" homes and also up in the Veteran's Hospital's Alcohol and Drug Unit. The homeless veteran program people *remembered that I once went through the VA homeless program myself*, and *now I was one of their success stories*. And *yes*, the Veterans Hospital spokesperson said they would *send me some* alcoholic homeless veterans needing sober living.

At one of my Friday night meetings, I had just posted up a flyer on their board; and a woman named Olivia came up to me and asked, "Hey, Stuart, if *you need a good lady manager* for your *women's sober living home, consider me!* I'm currently the manager of Cedarwood's Sober Living Home for women now, and I'll be *happy* to help get your place going in exchange for a free room. Also, my boyfriend *Harry* here is a *handyman*. He can fix *anything! He* can be your *men's house manager*. And Harry can bring his own pickup truck too!" (That pickup truck sure was needed!)

"Come on over. We will set things up," I said.

It was *another "godsend"* as Olivia and Harry were very good start-up managers. Olivia soon had the *Ladies Gone Sober* house filled up with five women. The flyers and efforts I made brought in five men, so Harry managed the *Sober Guys Men's House*. And he *loved fixing up stuff!* There was a never-ending list of things to do. Wow! This was good!

In a sober living home, the residents did all their own chores—cleaning, cooking, yard maintenance, etc.—just as if it were their own home because when you live at a sober living house, *it was your home* and others living there were your "family."

One day, the men were not doing the yard work. I called my AA lady friend, Lilly, who never wore a bra, to *rake the leaves*. Soon, all the male residents were helping her!

What was different about living together as a family at *my* sober living place was that my place was only for people who were *seri-*

ous about staying clean and sober and only people with the disability of chemical dependency (alcohol and/or other drug addiction). At Sobriety Castle, there was no recovery program counseling or any other services provided. The shared housing was run democratically by its residents, and all residents must maintain an *active* program of recovery by attending twelve-step meetings *daily*. Lucky for them, the local twelve-step meeting room was on our property, so they can walk to a meeting—no excuses.

And by now, I bought a new nine-passenger van, and even though daily twelve-step meetings were held on Sobriety Castle property in the meeting room, I'd load up my van and offer to take anyone who wanted to come to outside meetings within a thirty-mile radius, including other speaker meetings and twelve-step conventions at hotels in Palm Springs and San Diego. Also, recovering people have lots of social events, including dances, picnics, and camping. I took my residents to every place I could, and as a result, Sobriety Castle was getting a very good reputation with a very high rate of people staying sober. Things were going great!

One day, I got a phone call from Natasha, who was a counselor at Maplewood and, as you already knew, a close friend.

"What is it, Nattie?" I asked.

"Well, I called to ask you a favor, Stuart," she said. "This Saturday night, we have a panel coming in to speak to all our residents at once in the auditorium—fifty men and fifty women. All are newcomers. The panel leader is *Marcy from Los Angeles*."

"That sounds cool, Natasha," I replied. "Are you inviting me and my residents to come and listen?"

"No, Stuart, I'm inviting you and your best recovering residents to be on the panel with Marcy. She does not have enough people. I told her I would ask someone, and that some-one is you!" she said.

"*Count us in!*" I enthusiastically agreed.

So the next Saturday, I loaded the van with people I knew from my Castle twelve-step meeting, and some residents and I headed out to go on stage to do our first "outreach" panel.

Sitting up on stage at Cedarwood House facing one hundred newcomers in recovery was a wonderful experience. I brought eight people, and Marcy, the panel leader, brought four.

After hearing Marcy share her twelve-step story of experience, strength, and hope, I was blown away. She had eighteen years of sobriety and looked a lot like my wife, Maria—very pretty. Marcy was an *excellent* twelve-step speaker!

After each of us panel members talked three to four minutes to the newcomers, it was over, and the Maplewood House residents thanked us for volunteering to come out and share our stories.

After that twelve-step panel experience, Marcy said, "Hey, let's all go to Denny's for coffee!" So we did. We socialized and talked until midnight about the joys of living sober. I was becoming attracted to Marcy.

"So what other panels do you go to?" I asked Marcy.

"Well, Stuart," she answered, "I go to a lot of them. Do you want to be on my panel team?"

"Yes, I certainly do!" I said.

"Okay then!" Marcy happily answered. "Once a month, every third Saturday, bring *your people* by 6:30 p.m. in the Maplewood parking lot."

So the residents of Sobriety Castle also volunteered to reach out to other recovery centers on panels. Sobriety Castle residents attended our home group meeting daily. I went to all twelve-step conventions, and now we were participating in hospital and institution panels. We helped carry the message of recovery to many institutions—even to prisons and detention centers and the Salvation Army.

I always went with *Marcy*. She drove a Cadillac and worked in an office. I was finding myself being more and more attracted to her, and one day, I was *kidding around* about the future possibility of her hooking up some-day. Marcy stopped cold in her tracks. She put her hands behind my head and brought me face-to-face with her. *She looked me right in the eyes* and said, *"Stuart! Be very careful with what you wish for because you will get it! Do you understand me, Stuart?"*

That scared me. "Yes, I do, Marcy, loud and clear!" I said. And I *never* kidded around or flirted with her *ever again*.

Marcy said, "Stuart, I have *another* twelve-step panel. I need four more people willing to go with me. Can I count you in?"

"Where is this twelve-step panel going?" I asked.

"To downtown Los Angeles's *Skid Row!*" Marcy said. "I go every six months on a Monday night."

"Count me in!" I said.

I called my wife, Maria, and told her all about it (except for the 'kidding around with Marcy' part). I felt weird about going back to Skid Row again and asked Maria to come with me for company. I called Marcy and asked if my wife, Maria could come along.

"Yes, of course," she replied, "*but only* twelve-steppers can share."

"*No problem...thanks, Marcy,*" I said.

"God is awesome," Marcy said.

A car pool of four cars followed Marcy on a Sunday afternoon going to *the Skid Row Tumbleweed meeting* at a church courtyard located in the heart of *Skid Row* in the downtown LA area. My wife, Maria, had a couple of boxes of old clothes from our garage to give away free to the homeless people, which she did.

I became nervous when our four cars drove past hundreds of homeless people in the same area where I first found Brenda all those years ago. *I wonder if that cardboard box is still there?* I thought to myself.

Marcy parked her new Cadillac right in front of the church. So did we. Anyway, I was *terrified* of being back in that homeless area. *Sober, I'd never ever be in an area like that!*

The bottom line, it was one of the *best meetings* ever! That *Skid Row panel* in downtown LA was great! *I would never forget it—giving back for fun and for free!*

CHAPTER TWENTY-EIGHT

New Residents

SMOKEY the Sobriety Cat

Before I left home to go to my *other* bedroom at Sobriety Castle, my wife, Maria, suggested, "Why don't you bring your cat Smokey to the castle to stay with you there for company?"

"A cat wouldn't be safe out there from the coyotes unless I kept it *inside* my room," I explained.

"Well, that's *your* choice," Maria said.

My cat Smokey turned out to be *excellent* company and appreciated being inside my room and the center of my attention. And Smokey did *not even want to go outside*, except to take care of "natural" functions.

That cat was also a "watch cat." It could hear someone driving into the entrance of the long gravel driveway entrance up to a mile away or coming up *my path* to knock on my door much sooner and better than I could ever do.

My cat Smokey would *always* let me know by meowing loudly and incessantly when somebody was coming onto the property. Also, in the morning, Smokey would *paw* me when it was time for me to get up and comfort me by purring when I was upset or lonely. Smokey was *a good friend indeed*.

Besides *my* bedroom at Sobriety Castle, I had *another spare room* which we called a "God bed" for special guests like my family, of course. But more importantly, I reserved the room for *emergency housing* for down-and-out alcoholics.

I *selectively offered free temporary housing for people I picked up off the streets or elsewhere who wanted to go to rehab and get help* and could not do it by themselves.

The lady living there this night was Cindy, who was very thin and *dying* from AIDS. *She was a homeless veteran* whom I found begging for money outside a store. And tomorrow morning, I was bringing her *for treatment* at the local *Veteran's Hospital*. It was all arranged, and she got her help!

The phone rang. It was *Mary!* "Hi, Stuart," she said. "Just checking up on you and your cat. Do you have a new sponsor yet?"

"No, I'm still looking for one," I answered. "I need to talk about my issues...like *why* my daughter, Myra, still *never talks to me.*"

"Did you try making your amends to her yet?" Mary asked.

"Yes," I replied, "but it seems like it *did not work* as Myra is not responding. She still drinks too."

The 6:00 p.m. "happy hour" twelve-step meeting had just finished. I'd had a long day at my daytime office job, and it was a good meeting tonight.

It was about 8:00 p.m. I was lying down in my bedroom in Sobriety Castle, watching TV. Suddenly, my cat Smokey started meowing loudly. That meant someone was coming down my path to knock on my door. Now I could hear the footsteps. I had a brass knocker on my door.

Knock...knock...knock!

"Who is it?" I inquired cautiously.

Through my peephole, I could see it was one guy. I opened the door.

"Hi, what can I do for you, sir?" I said.

"I need to get admitted to your sober living home right now! My name is Tommy," the man said.

"Whoa, Tommy!" I answered. "Come back tomorrow during office hours, and we can talk about it then."

Mary said, "Making amends is done *for you*, not for her. You did *your* part. Whether she accepts it is up to *your Higher Power*. Stuart, I *identify with you* because *I have a daughter who does not talk to me either* and *never* forgave me from my *drinking days*. I was an unfit mother. She even changed her name, so I couldn't find her."

"Wow, how sad," I said.

Mary suggested, "Stuart, *I don't have a sponsor yet either*, so why don't we talk by phone to each other every day. And we can *co-sponsor each other* until we find ourselves *real* sponsors?"

So it came to pass that Mary and I phoned each other *daily*, and it *really helped* my twelve-step program and hers.

One day, a big rig truck pulled up and parked on the street next to our large white fence that was right in front of Sobriety Castle property. My cat *Smokey meowed*, and soon, a rough-looking gentleman knocked on my door, asking, "Are you the owner of this Sobriety

Castle sober living place? Hi...I'm a *friend of Bill W*. I'm Jack."

In twelve-step meetings, we tried to be *anonymous* and often referred to each other by our *first names only*, and sometimes, first names with the initial of our last names were used.

The *founder* of *Alcoholics Anonymous* wished that his *real name not be used*. So he referred to himself as "Bill W." So it came to pass that if you said, "I'm a friend of Bill W.," it was sort of a *secret code* not known to the general public, which was a way of telling people that *you were a member of Alcoholics Anonymous*. If the person did not have any idea of what you are talking about or asked, "Bill *who*?" then the person you were talking to probably wasn't a member of Alcoholics Anonymous or maybe wasn't even an alcoholic at all.

"Well, Jack, I'm also a *friend of Bill W.*," I said. "Are you looking for a twelve-step meeting? We have them right here!"

"No," said Jack, "I have over *twenty years of sobriety*. My wife and I are having a quarrel, so I'd like to stay at your sober living home for about six months. Your place has a *good reputation*! And *of course*, I go to meetings *all of the time*. And *you have meetings right here too*! *Your place is perfect*! It's a godsend for me. I can be a good example of sobriety for all your newcomer residents."

"Okay, Jack!" I announced. "You *can* come in as a resident. Welcome home, Jack!"

Jack moved in to his own room in building number 3.

Knock, knock again—it was Tommy!

"No, I can't come back later," Tommy explained hurriedly. "You see, *I'm on the run*! I have been sober for ninety days at another facility. *But I hate it there*, so I ran away from it."

"Okay, Tommy." I consented. "Go to the front meeting room. It's *empty* now. We will *talk about it*."

Tommy explained that his mother had *thirty years sobriety* in Alcoholics Anonymous. And Tommy said he wanted *no other* type of recovery program for himself, except working the twelve-steps in a twelve-step meeting like the serenity house advocated. Tommy revealed that he just got out of *prison* and he was in a halfway house doing "rational recovery."

People who had disabilities had them *not by choice*! And many people who, over time, had become chemically dependent or addicted *had lost the power of choice to stop without outside help*! Alcoholics Anonymous for example recognized *alcoholism* as an *incurable disease* as did the *American Medical Association*. Many Government programs still called it "alcohol and drug abuse," in which the language implied *blaming the victim for having a disease of addiction*! The stigmatization that resulted would imply that the person *abused something*; therefore, he or she must be a *bad* person for doing so. Hopefully, the more proper recognition of the term "alcohol and drug dependency" was now being taught in universities and medical schools and was slowly replacing the blame-the-victim descriptive term of alcohol and drug abuse.

The people at the halfway house were mean to Tommy too. Tommy saw a Sobriety Castle flyer posted on a bulletin board in a twelve-step club and grabbed it and ran away and came to my place because Sobriety Castle had a *good reputation*!

Tommy said, "I *know my probation officer is after me*, and I'll be thrown back in jail or prison when they catch me. But if I can get admitted into your place, my probation officer just *might let me stay here*! My mother will pay the monthly fee. Here is his phone number."

"Tommy, before I let you in, I need to ask you two questions," I said. "Are you a friend of Bill W.'s?"

"Yes, I am!" said Tommy enthusiastically.

"Right answer!" I replied encouragingly. "Second question, what is your *sobriety date*?" One of the most often asked questions of my residents and in twelve-step programs was what your sobriety date was. It was the *last day* you drank alcohol or took drugs. If you were truly clean and sober, you *always remem-*

bered your sobriety date or your last drink. In Alcoholics Anonymous, it was like your birthday when you were reborn into a new life, and yearly anniversaries were highly celebrated in twelve-step programs. If you didn't know your sobriety date, then you don't have one!

Tommy proudly stated his sobriety date, which was over ninety days ago. I discussed with Tommy what a sober living home was and what was expected of him. He said he would go to meetings every day here and that before he was relapsed and went to prison, he had ten years of sobriety.

"Listen, Tommy," I continued, "give me the name of your probation officer, and I'll phone him."

"Here is his card," Tommy said. "But I know for sure that the police are after me right now, and they are coming to take me away to prison."

I called Tommy's mother, and she *drove* over immediately and paid his monthly fee *in cash*. I called his probation officer and got an answering machine. So I left a message for Tommy's probation officer, explaining all about Sobriety Castle and that I'd interviewed Tommy and agreed he will do better staying at my sober living place.

So I let Tommy come in that night and showed him his room and gave him his keys.

"Your roommate has two years of sobriety. You will get along great!" I said.

Tommy said, "Thanks, Stuart, but I still think they are coming to take me back to prison."

"Go to sleep, Tommy," I suggested. "I'll phone your probation officer again tomorrow and take care of it."

I called Maria and told her all about it, and then I called my co-sponsor Mary to tell them. Just then, my cat Smokey was meowing her head off again.

"What is it this time, Smokey?" I asked my cat curiously. "It's about midnight, and it's pitch-black outside. I see no cars or people." I stared at Smokey, wondering what was going on in her head.

But Smokey was still meowing. She definitely heard something! I got my flashlight and walked out into my giant backyard. Something was making noise behind my shed.

My cat Smokey was standing in my doorway, silhouetted by my room light, as I walked into the darkness, following my beam of light.

On the side of my toolshed I saw a giant raccoon, and he was looking back at me with sad eyes. It looked as if he had been hurt as he was just lying there.

"What's the matter, big fellow?" I asked the raccoon. "Are you okay? I'm your friend, Stuart. I won't hurt you," I said in a soft voice.

It was a beautiful animal—the biggest raccoon I'd ever seen in my life. My guess was that it got hit by a car and crawled over from the main road to my shed, but now it needed help.

"Don't be afraid, Mr. Raccoon," I said gently. "Wait right here."

I got some cat dishes and put food and water dishes near the raccoon. Then I phoned the animal control center.

"I have a wonderful raccoon on my property," I reported. "It's a beautiful animal, and it's been injured. I want it to live and be relocated. Can you come and get it *right away*?"

Luckily, the animal control dispatcher was a sympathetic lady. "I'll send a wagon truck over first thing tomorrow morning to pick up the raccoon."

So now, it was morning, and I'd had my coffee. Smokey was up all night, worrying about how the raccoon was doing. The raccoon was still alive but lying there sadly. And then, a white *animal control wagon truck* pulled up in the driveway, then picked up the wounded raccoon and loaded him into the back.

"Thanks for picking him up," I said to the animal control rescue workers. "I hope that raccoon lives."

"We will try our best to save him, Stuart," the driver reassured me.

Just then, my newest resident Tommy ran up to us at the animal control truck.

"*I'm here to turn myself in,*" he said! "*I surrender!*"

"Tommy, relax!" I said. "This is not a parole wagon...it's an animal control truck! I phoned your probation officer this morning. He said *it's okay. You can stay here!* Now go back to your room and relax."

"Thanks, Stuart," said Tommy.

Tommy became *one of our best* twelve-step residents, and we had *another success story.*

About a month later, the animal control center called me up with miraculous news. He said, "The raccoon you rescued has fully recovered. We named him Bandito because as soon as he felt better, he started eating all of the other animals' food. He was healthy enough to release back to the County Wildlife Preserve. We had a big party for him and gave him a hug goodbye."

Tears came to my eyes. Had I not been sober, I would have never been able to save and prolong that precious racoon's life. *Sobriety really worked!*

CHAPTER TWENTY-NINE

Stuart Saves His Daughter

Tommy's probation officer drove out to Sobriety Castle Sober Living Homes and told me that my place had the best reputation for success stories relating to a number of people maintaining their sobriety.

Tommy's probation officer said, "Maybe I can send more people to live at your place!"

"Well, sir," I answered, "this is not a half-way house, nor is it a flophouse. All residents must have a chemical dependency issue and must be an active participant in their recovery, meaning that they need to attend twelve-step meetings if they choose to live here."

"*This is a good place!*" the official said. "I'll see what I can do!"

He drove away in his car.

It was Friday morning now at about 10:00 a.m. I was at my office job. My telephone rang. My Maria was calling me.

"Dear, it's Maria! Come *home* quick! Something is wrong with Myra."

Since I was kind of my own boss at my office job and had seniority. I could come and go as I pleased, and this day I did not have any clients scheduled to see me. Even if I did, *my family was my top priority*!

"I'm on my way, Maria," I said.

Back at my home, Maria was sitting in Myra's room. Myra seemed like she was in a lethargic coma, acting like a rag doll.

"How long has she been like this?" I asked Maria.

"All morning," Maria answered. "I can't get her to wake up!"

"Maria, Myra is sick," I said. "We don't know what is wrong. I'm taking her to the hospital! Come along!"

So my family got in the car. I carried Myra downstairs and carefully put her in the back seat next to my wife, Maria.

It felt *strange* driving to the hospital. At the *hospital emergency room*, there were about fifty others waiting for service, but when we carried her in and put her in a wheelchair, the hospital staff listened to Maria and me as we pleaded with them to give Myra immediate attention. They knew that Myra was in serious condition and, within moments, had her on a gurney with all kinds of monitors hooked up to her.

"Myra, this is your dad!" I shouted in anguish. "Hang in there! You're in a hospital. But I'll be around, and so will your family be here. You will be okay! *Hang in there, Myra!*"

The hospital staff consisted also of college students from a nearby medical college, and they used this hospital as a training center for their internships as they were soon to be doctors.

Before long, Myra was moved to the fifth floor of the hospital, and we all went up to visit her. The nurse told us, "Well...she is not conscious yet! We don't know what is wrong with her, but we think that she has septic toxic shock syndrome. It is very serious. We are running tests on her."

Myra had *even more machines*_hooked up to her and all kinds of plastic tubes going in and out of her.

It was about 4:00 p.m. now. My wife, Maria, and myself were at her bedside, comforting Myra.

The nurse said, "I'm sorry, but the doctors are going to do special tests. And visiting hours are over now. Trust me. Your daughter, Myra, will be okay. I'll keep an eye on her. You can all go home now."

I was at my wife's house and decided to stay around. The phone rang. Maria answered it. It was the hospital. They said to Maria, "Myra is *dying!* You'd better come quickly!"

Within minutes, Maria and I were back into my car and almost flying back to the hospital.

Within seconds, the two of us are in a doorway of a "code blue" room with about eight people surrounding Myra!

A student lady doctor spoke to Maria and me. "I'm sorry," she said. "Your daughter's gone. We have been working on her for more than fifteen minutes. Her heart has stopped. I'm sorry."

My eyes focused on a man in the middle of the crowd around the bed where Myra was. He was trying to use CPR to bring Myra back.

"Don't stop! Keep on going!" I screamed. "I *know* my daughter. She is a fighter! She *will* come back! What's fifteen minutes? Don't you get paid by the hour? Keep going!"

My wife, Maria, was in shock. She couldn't believe that the lady doctor had said to her that Myra was dead.

"Myra!" I shouted. "I know Myra. She doesn't know all these strangers. She knows *us*! She will listen to *us*! Maria, go to the other side of the bed and talk to her! Myra! This is your dad! I love you! Come on, wake up! Now come on!" I said loudly and emphatically.

Then the voices of myself and Maria loudly cheered Myra on! It was twenty-five minutes now—still no heartbeat. I was intently watching the man doing CPR, and suddenly a miracle happened! It worked! Myra's heart started beating again. She was alive! The whole room started cheering!

But the lady student doctor said to me, "Yeah, but even if she lives, she might have brain damage."

I took that lady aside and said to her, "Listen, lady, if you're going to be a doctor, you need to have a *more positive attitude!*" PACE = Positive attitude changes everything.

Myra was moved to another room. Only this time, I laid it down to the hospital staff, "My family and I are staying in the room with Myra twenty-four hours a day from now on until she is released from this hospital! She almost died! We want to stay nearby because she will respond better to us than to strangers. *We know our daughter!*"

The hospital official said, "Okay, but only one family member at a time can stand watch over her unless it's during visiting hours."

Maria and I took turns, four- to eight-hour shifts, watching Myra. We did this for three weeks. Myra got better and did not have any brain damage. She was fine! Maria was in the hospital room when Myra spoke again.

Myra asked, "Where's Dad?"

Maria called me at Sobriety Castle.

"Tell her Dad's on the way, Maria," I said. And I drove immediately to see her.

Now Maria told me that had I been my old drunken self and not had been sober today, Myra would have died. Maria said I saved Myra's life. But I knew better. God did.

"Thank you, Higher Power!" I said with deepest gratitude and humility.

We later learned that in the history of that hospital, no one has ever lasted twenty-five minutes before without a heartbeat and had come back to life.

The man doing the CPR was promoted, first as a CPR instructor and later as the head of his entire department! A year later, I drove my family back, and we made a plaque to honor the man. Thanked him. It was a very good day!

I realized that sobriety had rewards that I had never even dreamed of. And I thanked my Higher Power for that!

CHAPTER THIRTY

San Diego

The "Big" Convention

Myra got better, and her memory *was fine*. Myra was *never* an alcoholic; so she was *smarter than me*, who caused my own self to have brain damage as a result of *my excessive drinking*.

I was happy and sober for sixteen years now, and there were lots of *social events* put on by twelve-step groups all year round.

It was the *month of May* now, and I saw an announcement flyer about a big twelve-step convention to be held at a fancy hotel in San Diego this month. My sweet wife, Maria, and I decided that we needed some *quality time together*; so I suggested to Maria, "Let's go to the *San Diego AA convention*. It is at the Goodview Hotel *right by the ocean and boardwalk area*! We can have a fun weekend together!"

The information flyer about the twelve-step convention said there were two main speakers, both from out of state. The Friday night speaker was a guy from New Jersey, and the Saturday night speaker was a lady from Texas.

So I reserved a place for the Friday night *fancy dinner* for my wife and me. The *dinner* would be followed by listening to the main speaker from New Jersey. So it sounded like fun!

There was a "donation fee" at AA conventions to *pay* for the *dance bands*, the *comedy shows*, and the *fancy dinners* as all this cost money. But the beautiful and wonderful part of all this was that *the AA meetings* themselves, according to the *twelve traditions* of Alcoholics Anonymous, *should always be free* to attend to *any alcoholic* in need of a meeting. If this tradition of free meetings was not followed, you would just have a bunch of rich old-timers talking to themselves, *helping no one*, and then the message of recovery would not be heard. The *newcomers* were the *most important persons*.

Maria and I arrived Friday night at the Goodview Hotel and checked into our luxurious hotel room and opened the room curtains to a *gorgeous view of the Pacific Ocean* on one side and the boardwalk with little shops, boutiques, and restaurants on the other. "Wow! This is great!" I said to Maria.

I bought a local San Diego newspaper because we were not sure what we would do *Saturday night*. So we looked to see what was going on this weekend in San Diego. And then, *I saw it*.

"Wow!" I exclaimed. "Maria, look at this! *Guess* who is in town having a concert *tomorrow night*?"

"Who?" Maria asked me.

"It's *Joan Baez* in concert this Saturday night in the San Diego all-star outdoor motel, Theater Under the Stars, tomorrow night."

"Maria, *I want to go!*" I told her. "Because I want to meet her and ask her about the time way back in the sixties, more than forty years ago, when I was in a *Greenwich Village* coffeehouse, and I heard her marvelous voice! I *wonder* if it was really her and if she *remembered me!*"

"Of course she would remember you, Stuart," Maria said confidently. "You are unforgettable! Maybe if you can remind her what you were wearing that evening..."

"I remember!" I announced. "I was wearing my sailor suit! How could I ever forget such a thing? Of course she will remember me! Maria, I just have to find Joan Baez and make her remember me! I was her biggest fan back then, and maybe I still am! Nobody can sing as beautifully as she can!"

"Well, Stuart," she answered, "Joan Baez is a *beautiful* singer, and it seems to mean a lot to you to go. So I'm *okay with it*! The tickets are only twenty-five dollars."

I called up the outdoor theater.

"Sorry, we are completely *sold out*!" the ticket agent for the theater said.

"Sold out?" I replied in extreme disappointment. "This cannot be true!"

"Yes, two weeks ago we sold out," said the ticket agent. "But several minutes ago, there came available *one cancellation* for two *premium front row seats* in our *exclusive motel concert* deal."

"Only *two seats available*?" I asked in bewilderment. "How much will *that* cost?"

"*Five hundred dollars each!*" she said. "For two, that's *one thousand dollars*. But your motel room *overlooks* the outdoor theater under the stars. *Plus, you have front row seats!*"

Maria said, "We can't afford it, Stuart. No way, Stuart!"

"But this is a *once-in-a-lifetime opportunity*, Maria," I pleaded. "*Maybe I can meet Joan Baez* and finally ask her...it's a dream come true!" I said.

"I'm *not sure about this*," said Maria. "But *if it will make you happy, go ahead* and book the room and tickets for tomorrow night to see Joan Baez." I bought the tickets.

That Friday night, we were at the AA convention called "The Friends of Bill W." It was fun, mingling and chatting with over a thousand other alcoholics there—all *dressed up*! Almost all the attendees there, although you'd never guess by looking at them, were alcoholics.

We sat at our reserved AA dinner table with our ticket seat numbers with a good view of the stage, where later the main speaker would appear.

After we ate a fifty-dollar dinner, some readings were read out loud. Then, the meeting leader spoke into the microphone, "Ladies and gentlemen, tonight, it is my honor and privilege to introduce our main speaker, who flew all the way from New Jersey to be with us this fine Saturday evening. Here is Harry Jones with twenty-eight years of sobriety!"

Everyone clapped and cheered as the speaker told us about his recovery experiences, and he had a good sense of humor, starting his talk with a few jokes. He was dressed in a suit and tie, looking really sharp.

Then suddenly, Harry spoke very loudly into the microphone. "There are *two* kinds of people in this room, and *you* know who *you* are. Half of *you* are convicted felons! And the other half of you people in this very audience are *unconvicted felons*!"

The audience was spellbound by Harry's speech as he continued. "But that was your old life before you got sober and worked your recovery program. I remember, *long ago*, I was a *daily drunk*, and I used to be a *state senator*. One day, after half a bottle of scotch, some guys came into my office, all dressed up as Arabs. We all had a few drinks, and next thing I knew, I ended up in prison. Go figure!"

"Wow," I said, "I sure hope nothing like that ever happens to me," I said.

After the speaker finished, Maria and I went up to our hotel room and held each other tight and enjoyed looking at the moonlight across the ocean. And we slept together in a luxurious *giant king-sized bed. We were very happy!*

"It doesn't get any better than *this*, my love Maria!" I said adoringly.

"Well, that's true, Stuart," she replied. But remember, *tomorrow* is a big day *for you too*. Remember, we are going to the Joan Baez concert!"

Before leaving the Goodview Motel, I went to a 6:00 a.m. marathon meeting, and then back to my hotel room. Maria slept until 10:00 a.m.

We checked out of the hotel and had fun walking on the ocean beach and looking at the little tourist shops along the boardwalk.

"Well, Maria," I said, "Let's go to the all-star outdoor motel theater and check into our room." So we checked in. I asked the desk clerk, "I'm hoping I can actually meet Joan Baez. These *are* expensive tickets."

"Well," he said, "I can't promise you anything, but this afternoon, her stage crew will be setting up. *Maybe they* will help you find a way to meet Joan Baez."

CHAPTER THIRTY-ONE

The Joan Baez Concert

My wife, Maria, and I had moved into our exclusive and expensive *motel room* at San Diego's all-star motel, Theater Under the Stars, and down the hallway and down the stairs led to the back of the concert stadium, where Joan Baez would be singing tonight.

The vendor was setting up a Joan Baez *souvenir* stand, and the band setup team was up on the stage, setting up loudspeakers and equipment.

Yes, I was able to roam about unattended and freely around the empty stadium theater when it was closed because I was *staying* at this exclusive motel. The side gate entrance for the public to come this evening was still closed.

The backstage entrance gate was tall and large and made out of wooden logs.

I was wearing one of my very own *Sobriety Castle T-shirts* that I had made for the twelve-step convention. I went back to the room and checked in with Maria.

"What's up, Stuart?" Maria asked.

"Well, they are setting up for Joan's concert tonight, but there is *no sign* of Joan rehearsing or anything!"

"Why don't we just *relax* and *enjoy* the show tonight. We have *great* seats!" suggested Maria.

"But I'm obsessed with the idea that I might be able to meet this singer, Joan Baez, whom I adore, finally after more than forty years," I explained to my dear wife. "Maria, I'll be right back," I said.

I went over to the very busy gentleman that was setting up the souvenir booth for tonight's concert. I *already had_*almost *all* of Joan's recorded songs, but there *were* a *few* I hadn't heard yet. So I bought some concert souvenir items: three Joan Baez T-shirts for my wife, Maria and my daughter, Myra.

No one else was at the stand yet because it was not open to the public yet. I asked the vendor, "Say, *buddy*, as you can guess, I am a *big fan* of Joan's and have been *all these past forty years*. And long ago, I met her. Do you think that *you* could help me get *backstage* after the concert and meet Joan?"

The vendor was unloading boxes and stacking up more T-shirts on the table. "Listen, pal," the vendor answered, "I only *work here*, and Joan has just come back flying in from another country. She is tired, so I don't think she'll want to be greeting her fans tonight. Sorry, pal. Can't help ya!"

"But," he added, "you might go over to the stage and ask the *stage manager, Bennie*, to see if *he* can get you in to meet Joan."

I walked through the empty concert stadium, through the center aisle, down past a hundred rows of empty chairs.

I saw the crew in black T-shirts setting up the gear and checking to see if the microphones were working yet.

"Excuse me!" I shouted to someone on stage. "Can I speak to Bennie?"

"I'm Bennie. What can I do for you?"

"Well, sir, I'm staying at this motel," I answered, pointing and saying, "See, there is my wife, Maria, up there in the window."

Maria waved, and Bennie waved back.

"Well, Bennie," I continued, "it's been my life's dream to get backstage and say hello to Joan Baez. I met her years ago and want to see if she remembers me. Can you tell her that Stuart from forty years ago is here to see her?"

Bennie looked at me as if I were crazy.

"Stuart, tell you what," Bennie replied, "there is a busload of the Joan Baez fan club coming in later today. And they will line up outside backstage at the entrance gate after the concert. So after the concert, just go over and stand in line with them."

"Thanks, Bennie!" I said. *He's not going to help me either*, I thought. *What's wrong with these guys?*

"Well, how did it go?" Maria asked me.

"Well, maybe I can meet her. I don't know. If I do get in later, I'll come back and get you," I explained.

"Stuart, let's relax now," she said encouragingly. "There are only two more hours."

I took Maria down to the motel's restaurant, and indeed, there were some Joan Baez fan club members there. It looked like a bunch of middle-aged hippies, not unlike myself. More women than men were there.

They had all kinds of T-shirts and buttons from other Joan Baez concerts. I spoke with one lady who told me that she followed Joan all over the country, going to every one of her concerts.

"That's great!" I said. "What is that *purple wristband* you're wearing?"

"That's so later tonight we can get back on our bus and head back to Los Angeles," she explained. "We'll see you at the concert," she added.

"Nice meeting you," I said.

Maria and I were now in our front row seats, and before I knew it, standing there, less than twenty feet in front of me, was the female singer I idolized for *all these years*: *Joan Baez*! It was a magical moment!

I was in a trance of disbelief during the whole concert. She sang the most melodic songs, from "Love Is Just a Four-Letter Word" to protest songs from the sixties, like "With God on Our Side." I thoroughly enjoyed the concert, and so did my wife, Maria.

The Joan Baez concert was *now over*. She was gone. The stadium which was once full was now empty. Maria told me, "I'm tired, Stuart. I'll wait in our motel room. You go ahead and see if you can meet her. I love you."

"Thanks, Maria, for your love and understanding," I said tenderly.

Over by the tall wooden backstage gate were about sixty people waiting to see Joan. Security guards were letting people in one by one, but I was noticing everyone was not being let in. Now my turn came.

"Where are *you* going?" the guard asked.

"Why, to meet Joan Baez, of course. The stage manager, Bennie, told me to get in *this line* after the concert." I looked up to the stage. Everyone up there, including Bennie, was *gone!*

"That's all fine and dandy," said the guard, "but do you have a purple wristband of the Joan Baez fan club?"

"No, I don't," I replied honestly.

"Then you can't come backstage," he said.

Soon, the large log doors to the backstage area shut, and there were about twenty of us Joan Baez fans who had been refused entrance backstage to see her.

What would Joan do? I thought.

"Hey, everyone!" I shouted. *"What would Joan do? Would she give up? Heck no! She would protest!"*

So we all started chanting out loud: *"We want Joan! We want Joan! We want Joan!"*

"What's going on here?" asked the guard.

"We are not leaving until we get backstage and see Joan Baez!" I said, with the crowd cheering me on and repeating the very same thing.

"Sorry!" the guard yelled back. "Everyone has to leave now! The concert is over! The theater is closed!"

So next, we all sat down and chanted: *"Hell no! We won't go! Hell no! We won't go!"*

And then we all started singing "We Shall Overcome!"

"Look," I said to another can't-get-backstage-to-see-Joan-Baez protester, "the guard is calling someone on his walkie-talkie. He is probably talking to Joan herself, and I know she will let us in"

Just then, from the main entrance of the concert, the San Diego riot police came running up to us with shields, masks, and all kinds of mean- and nasty-looking equipment.

I got up and told my fellow protesters, "Good concert, but it's time to go home."

We were all escorted out into the street of the concert premises, but since I was staying at the motel, I went back into the front motel entrance back to my room. Maria was sleeping, but when I opened the door, she awakened.

"What happened, Stuart?" Maria asked.

"Nothing at all, my dear," I said. Except I just learned another lesson in sobriety—I was being selfish and self-centered. I learned that I could no longer *live in the past*. Everything I needed to be happy was right here right now *in front of me*. "Maria, it's you," I said. "I've been an *idiot* all weekend. Just being with you is all I need to *make me happy*."

The rest of the weekend, we went to Balboa Park in San Diego and had a wonderful time. And I never let Maria out of my sight or out of my arms, not even for *one moment*!

CHAPTER THIRTY-TWO

Meet the Mayor

Maria and I returned from a most wonderful weekend—a mini vacation for us. Even if it was only for a couple of days, we made the most of it.

I was back at Sobriety Castle now. Since allowing Tommy to come in, his parole officer had told other parole and probation officers about the good recovery program that I offered people by supporting twelve-step programs by *strongly_*suggesting to my residents that they attended them.

And referrals came in so fast I had trouble trying to find out which parolees were *really* and *truly* wanting help with alcohol and drugs and which just needed a "paper address," just having a place to stay with *no intention* at all of going to twelve-step meetings or any of the recovery programs.

"Are you a friend of Bill W.'s?" was a common question I asked of parolees interviewed. Only about one in ten could give the correct answer. So most parolees and probation refer-rals *were not accepted* into Sobriety Castle because they were not people with a disabil-ity of chemical dependency. We tried not to allow more than 50 percent of residents to be from the system.

In addition to my sober living home, other business-minded people thought that open-ing a sober living home would be a fast and easy way to make money off the system. Soon, there were other houses who called them-selves sober living houses all over town, trying to compete with me. Only one other that I knew had a twelve-step meeting place near their location, and some so-called sober living homes were, in truth and in fact, nothing more than flophouses, where everyone in them was *still using alcohol and drugs.*

Soon, the Sober Living Association monthly meeting became aware of the problem of these *bogus* sober living homes. And the topic of sober living homes became a political issue to our town and county.

There was a county judge named Judge Hawkins who was in *favor* of sober living homes and twelve-step programs for alcohol and drug and other addiction offenders.

Since I was the "community liaison" for the Sober Living Homes County Association, I invited Judge Hawkins to be our next *guest speaker* at our next monthly Sober Living Association meeting.

"Hi, everyone! I'm Judge Hawkins," the judge announced. "Thanks for inviting me to speak, Stuart. My first announcement to all of you is yes, I support quality *sober living homes* like yours and twelve-step programs. Secondly, I am announcing *today at your meeting* my intention to run for *mayor* of this city!"

Everyone in the room cheered and gave Judge Hawkins a standing ovation. Then Judge Hawkins continued by saying, "My mayoral opponent, Mr. John Taggit, the district attorney, is *opposed* to all sober living homes and wants to shut them all down, and in fact, he is doing it already! And if and when I am elected as your mayor, I will only support homes that are in fact members of *your* county Sober Living Association and who *follow* your inspection guidelines and your code of ethics just like *your model sober living home*, Sobriety Castle. Keep up the good work, Stuart!"

The back fence of Sobriety Castle could be seen by five hundred thousand passing cars per week. For the next few months, a large banner was mounted high, which read, "Hawkins for Mayor!"

When election day finally came, Judge Hawkins became Mayor Hawkins, and I was among the crowd watching the vote tally coming in that night. He won by a landslide vote!

"Congratulations, Mayor Hawkins," I said.

Mayor Hawkins kept his word, and I attended a monthly meeting downtown in the mayor's office, along with other Sober Living Association members, talking about how to best handle parolees and probation people who *did* have an alcohol and drug problem.

Mayor Hawkins's former opponent, District Attorney John Taggit, was still against sober living homes until Natasha said to me, "Don't worry, Stuart. I used to *date* John Taggit, and he is happily married but still wants me to see him. And we are *good friends* today. And I am starting a sober living home for women, so he *will* support us. I promise you, Stuart!"

It was obvious that I had many sober friends out there who had grown into positions of influence. But there was one more request from Mayor Hawkins' office to the coalition, and that was to *convince the town hall city council members* of the value of *quality sober living homes* in the community.

So Mayor Hawkins said to me, "Since your sober living home is one of the best, we want *you* to *talk* to the *town council* this Friday night, Stuart! And by the way, *you will be on live television—Public Access Channel 3!*"

I dressed up in a suit and tie, and I went to the civic center to City Hall through the oversized double doors leading to the Town Council Chambers. About five other Sober Living associates were there, also to speak on behalf of the benefits of sober living.

I saw the TV cameras. *Wow! I'm going to be on television!* I thought. I called my wife, Maria to tell her.

"I'm sorry, Stuart. I can't watch it. I'm at work," she said sadly.

I also phoned everyone I knew. No one was home or could watch me on TV. *I was the next speaker!* Then, my cell phone *rang.* I stepped outside to talk.

"Hey, this is Lilly. I'd like to help clean up your yard this Saturday and catch a meeting with you. Is that okay, Stuart?"

"*Hey, Lilly*, are you at home now?" I replied.

"Yes, I am," Lilly answered. "Why do you ask?"

"Because I'm at *City Hall*, about to go on *Public Access TV Channel 3!*" I said. "I'm going to be on right now! I'm on TV, Lilly. Turn on your set!"

"Stuart, I got you!" Lilly acknowledged. "I'll turn it on right now!"

Now, I don't remember one solitary word that I said up there; but I spoke very well, I was told later. The only person I knew in the county that actually saw me up there was my AA friend, Lilly.

"You were *fabulous*, Stuart!" she said.

CHAPTER THIRTY-THREE

The Odds Are Good

Back at Sobriety Castle, I got a phone call from a parole officer.

"Mr. Macpherson, I wonder if you could do me a big favor," he said. "I want you to allow someone in who is a big celebrity. He is a *famous rock star*."

"Listen," I told him, "at our sober living home, we tell nothing about anyone who lives here, and even who doesn't live here. We protect everyone's anonymity."

"Yes, we know that, Stuart," the parole officer said. He is a celebrity on parole. He got involved with one of his teenage groupies, and no one wants to let him into their sober living homes."

"What kind of recovery program does he have?" I asked. "We could *only* accept him if he is really an alcoholic or other chemically dependent person with a problem. He has to have more than ninety days of sobriety right now. He has to demonstrate that he is working on an active program of recovery. We were doing fine before without any parolees, and if I do let him in, he has to attend twelve-step meetings every day. And I need an agreement with you that if he messes up, I can call you and you'll haul him away. Those would be my conditions, and also all the other residents must see him too and approve him."

So it came to pass that Robbie, "The Rockin' Rabbit," a heavy metal guitar player, was allowed in as a resident. Everyone, including me, was a bit concerned about what kind of recovery program he had, but it turned out he had been to twelve-step meetings before.

Robbie soon said, "It's a godsend that I am here. *Meetings every day is exactly what I need.* I'm forever grateful for you letting me in when no one else would, Stuart. Thank you!"

During the next six months, Robbie attended meetings daily, never missing even one, and cheerfully did chores more than other residents. Even Lilly volunteered to come help with yard work more because Robbie was there. He even played at a concert on a stage where the Ren fair had been. He had recorded several music CDs, and sometimes he paused and sang for the other residents of Sobriety Castle.

So this Friday night, we decided to go into the Alano Club a couple of towns away because after the twelve-speaker meeting, there was a dance.

Robbie had nine months of sobriety now, and he was letting everyone know that he was God's gift to women. Only he thought so. We arrived at the twelve-step club. And yes, there were lots of women, and Robbie was immediately attracted to the sexiest-looking lady there. I was there with Robbie and six newer residents.

The sexy lady knew what was going on, and she winked at me. She was a long-time sober friend of mine.

Robbie boldly went up to the sexy lady and said to her, "Hi there, beautiful! I'm Robbie the Rockin' Rabbit. *You and I* are going to be together tonight!"

The lady grabbed Robbie by the front of his shirt and looked him right in the eyes. "You may be right, Robbie," she answered. "But first I have a question for you. What is *your* sobriety date?"

"I have nine months," Robbie feebly responded.

She put him down. "Try again, Robbie, in a couple of years when you have some *sobriety* under your belt! Robbie, see that guy over there?" She pointed to me. "He's been coming to meetings for years, and he *knows* how to *respect* women. It's something that *you* have yet to learn."

Just then, the lady shouted and pointed to Stuart. "Hey, *you* over there!"

"Yes," I said.

"Come on over. *Let's dance!*"

"Okay," I said.

Robbie went back with the newcomers and watched in amazement as the pretty lady was hugging and kissing me and dancing.

"How'd *he* do that?" asked Robbie.

I whispered in her ear, "*Thanks*, Dolores!"

Now Dolores was not trying to be unkind to newcomers; but with little or no experience at living a clean and sober life, it recommended *at least one year of sobriety, or even more time*, until a newcomer was *emotionally ready* for a *romantic relationship.*

Yes, there was an unofficial step called "step 13" or the "thirteenth step," where fooling around, flirting, and having sex occurred, and I had *no opinion* about that topic as long as people involved were able to *maintain sobriety.* It was often said that the two most common things that *drove* a person back to drinking alcohol or using other drugs were (1) romance and (2) finance.

So Dolores was showing Robbie that *she needed to be respected* because in the twelve-step program, with an endless list of sober and clean friends, all your needs, whatever they may be, would be taken care of.

So it was true, what Marcy said: "Be *very careful* what you wish for because you will get it."

So in other words, people's emotions were *not* to be messed with! I myself had learned that just having women as friends was great, even if no sex occurred. I discovered: "What a concept! Women as just friends!" Women were pretty "neat" people.

At a meeting, once I heard: "If you're looking for a real relationship at twelve-step meetings, the odds are good, but quite often the goods are odd!"

People in recovery may be a little "odd" and crazy, but we work *daily* to overcome our character defects and to be of maximum service to other people and to our Higher Power.

I asked Dolores, "Hey, Dolores, you are usually not at this twelve-step club. What brings you here tonight?"

"Well," she said, "*my* sponsor is tonight's *main speaker*, Mary Ann, who is a world champion women's ice skater. *She has over thirty-one years of sobriety.*"

Just then, a *very pretty lady*, looking like Marilyn Monroe, walked by the newcomers. They were in *awe* of *her beauty!* They were *stunned!* Dolores shared with me a secret: Mary Ann's real age was *seventy years old!*

That just went to show you what ongoing and continuous sobriety could do!

CHAPTER THIRTY-FOUR

The Last Trip

Sobriety Castle Sober Living Home was running at 80 percent capacity. I had applied at my job for a supervisory position. I had also been elected to be shop steward for my fellow counselors. I was sober for eighteen years now, and I'd never had it so good.

Maria called me. "I called Mexico to see how your brother Fred was doing. He has been ill for a few months, and his wife Janet says that he is not doing okay at all."

Stuart Visits His Dying Brother

Now, I loved my brother who was seventeen years older than me. He was eighty years old now, on his deathbed from smoking cigars. I told him years ago he might get throat cancer, and that was exactly what he got. He was dying from throat cancer. He was also a "social drinker." You'd have a drink. So shall I. Anyway, I did try to get him into a twelve-step program, but even though his own son died from alcohol poisoning, he would not listen or stop drinking.

But now, he was dying. So I could never tell him, "I told you so," even though I thought that. Unlike my brother Fred who flew his own airplane, I was deathly afraid of heights. Fred's wife, Janet, and I were like-minded in that regard. She would never set foot in an airplane. I had a fear of heights and of falling from high places. As a former house painter, I still feared ladders.

I had not seen my brother for ten years since he came to visit me. One thing was he had a fancy house in a gated community. It was as if he took his house in Santa Barbara and moved it to Mexico. The first thing my brother wanted the builders to do was make sure that there was a large bar to serve liquor. So that idea kept me away even though my brother mentioned that in his town there were a lot of retired Americans and Canadians living there, and to his surprise and mine, there was a twelve-step club in this town in Mexico.

So when my wife told me, "He may be dying," I said to her, "We're going right away this weekend." Even though I didn't want to fly on an airplane, we got us on the Friday night flight to Mexico. So my Maria and I boarded a plane, and I told her, "Well, this is one way to keep me talking to my Higher Power. I am really powerless now. I hope this plane does not crash!" I was sober now, trusting my Higher Power.

But the plane did not crash. We arrived in Guadalajara early in the morning. A rental car was waiting for us. We did not tell my brother and his wife that we were coming.

Back at Sobriety Castle before I left for my trip, my daughter, Myra, informed my wife and I that some guy got her pregnant. Of all things to happen! I was thinking, *What kind of creepy guy is she hooking up with?* I dreaded meeting this character who would be the father of my grandchild. I told Myra, "Well, we love you, and we will help you any way we can. You've been there for us, and we are here for you."

So Myra told us, "You know what? I talked to my boyfriend Jocko, and he wants to meet you both. What's more, he says he will voluntarily stay at Sobriety Castle and run it while you're gone."

So I was thinking, *What does this guy look like? My daughter, Myra, is a drinker, and Jocko is also a drinker.*

Myra said, *"Hey, Dad! I'm ready to stay sober and go to meetings! Don't worry…"*

So I met Jocko, and he was a tall very handsome guy and very nice. I told him, "Hey, this place is a sober living home—no drinking."

And for an unknown reason, Jocko said, "It's a good thing for me. I went to a meeting before, but this is the answer to my prayers.

Maybe by running Sobriety Castle, working with others, and going to meetings, I can stay sober," said Jocko. "I'll do my best."

So before my Mexico trip, I showed Jocko the ropes—all the meetings I went to, all the organizations. I went to even take him to the mayor's office, where I went to official meetings. Jocko soaked up all this information like a sponge. I told Jocko, "Well, I don't know exactly when I will return."

Jocko said, "As long as it takes until you return, I'll run your place, so don't worry." Well, I had to listen. He was family now—the father of my granddaughter.

Maria and I arrived in the Mexican town where my brother lived. Maria was born in Mexico and spoke fluent Spanish, so it was easy for us to get around. We found a map, looking up where my brother's place was. I also looked at an address I had in my pocket in order to locate and find out where the twelve-step meeting was located. I was stressed out and needed a meeting. So we found both addresses on the map. First, I found where the twelve-step meetings were—on a skinny side road on a boarded-up place which said "Club 12," so I knew that this was the right place. So next, we found a motel near the bottom of the road that would be leading up to my brother's gated community.

After settling in our Mexico motel room, we grabbed some food at an outdoor food stand. Good thing Maria spoke Spanish. The food was good!

It was Saturday morning at 11:00 a.m. So now we were driving in Mexico up a hill on a winding road with a view of Lake Chapalla. We approached a guardhouse in our rented car.

I told the guard, "Yes, I am looking for Fred and Janet. I am Fred's brother."

"Oh, yes!" said the guard. "We have been expecting you!"

He pointed to where the home was and told us the house number. We drove in, and the gates closed behind us!

Maria asked me, "How can anyone be expecting us? We didn't tell Janet and Fred that we are coming. We just came."

I said, "*I don't know!*"

We drove up to the house and parked. It was very nice—sunny sky, a beautiful location, a nice house, a nice view of the lake below.

We knocked on the door. Janet answered. She was surprised to see us. She said, "I was expecting *my* brother."

Now, I had not seen Janet's brother since I was a kid and he was a kid. He was now a retired naval officer and a college professor. And of course, a social drinker like his sister. His name was Charley.

So we were welcomed into my brother's retirement home. Maria told Janet to relax and asked if she could help out. Janet said yes. Soon, we saw where my brother was—in a bedroom with tubes and monitors hanging all over him attended by a private nurse. It did not look good.

I went in privately to see if I could speak to him and if he could wake up. "Hey Fred, this is your brother. Hello, anybody in there?"

His eyes opened, and he saw me. He looked happily surprised to see me. But he could not speak due to his throat cancer, but I could read his thoughts in his eyes. I said, "Hey, I told you I'd come to see you someday, and here I am. You know Janet is not the only one that has a brother—you do too!"

He smiled and mumbled a reply. Sounded like he tried to make a brotherly wisecrack back to me. But we were both happy to see each other. Then Maria came in, and we both talked to Fred. And he was very happy to see us, and it made the whole trip worthwhile to say our goodbyes.

So we made good company with Janet while Fred went back to sleep. We talked over old times and good memories. The time was now about three thirty. The doorbell rang. It was Janet's brother Charley. So we went for dinner and talked over old times. Since Charley and I were both in the US Navy once (me as an enlisted man and he as an officer), we all got to know each other better. It was a magical family reunion—a bittersweet happy time.

I looked at the clock and told them I needed to go somewhere for a while. I told them I needed to go to my twelve-step meeting. They said okay. I "saluted" Charley and left.

I drove up to the skinny driveway and parked near Club 12. I waited. The door was locked. Some other guy came driving up and parked. He got out and said, "Hi, I am Bruce. Is this where the meeting is?" So Bruce and I started having a meeting of our own. He was from Canada and had thirty-five years of sobriety. Twenty minutes later, other people came, and it was a good meeting made up of retired Americans and Canadians. They asked me to share maybe because I was new there, and I told them about my brother on his deathbed. Some said they knew who he was, and they all made me feel better and emotionally supported. Now, even if Janet and Charley had a drink, which they did, I did not have any need for it.

CHAPTER THIRTY-FIVE

Stuart's Last Meeting

The weekend would be over soon. Maria had to leave Monday. On Sunday morning, a twelve-step meeting was in a restaurant. So we went. It was upstairs and was a breakfast meeting. Maria was told she could not attend because that meeting was only for alcoholics and was not an "open meeting."

I almost got mad and walked out. But resentment was a number one offender, and I needed a meeting. Maria sat in a window booth downstairs in the restaurant. I ordered breakfast for her. All of a sudden outside, parade music was heard. I loved parades. A circus was in town. Unlike in the USA, the circus animals were not in cages but walking around on the street. What an interesting sight it was!

So Maria ate breakfast, watching the parade, with zebras and camels walking by her window. I went upstairs to my twelve-step meeting and closed the door. Time for us to go home. Stuart talked to his brother. Maria flew home on Monday morning. Maria went to Sobriety Castle. I was leaving on the Monday night flight. My plane lifted off into a hailstorm.

Something was wrong with my plane! The engine was sputtering. The plane crashed into the mountains of Mexico!

* * *

Maria arrived home safely. Her husband, Stuart, was missing in the crash and disappeared into fog and rain. Jocko and Myra had a daughter. Sobriety Castle Sober Living Home was doing okay, and so were the twelve-step meetings.

Myra went to sleep that night and had a dream.

"It's Dad!" she dreamed.

He had climbed up onto a ladder miles high from the ground, way up into the clouds. He was at the top rung of the ladder. The sky was stormy—lightning flashes, wild wind, rain, thunder.

Stuart cried out in the rain and fog. "Help me!"

"I'll help you!" said *Queen Anne's Ghost*. "Rise now and come with me, *Stuart MacPherson*"

The End

AFTERWORD

Hey! You, at the end of *this book, reading right now*! Thank you!

My mission is to *help people who want to get and stay sober*! And I have no opinion on outside issues. I hope you have enjoyed reading my book and that you have gained some insight into recovery that you did not know before.

Thanks so much for buying my book!

Founders of
ALCOHOLICS
ANONYMOUS
BILL W. & DR. BOB

REFERENCES FOR HELP
WITH ADDICTIONS

Alcoholics Anonymous
Post Office Box 459
475 Riverside Drive
New York, NY 10015
Phone (212) 870-3400
Fax (212) 870-3003
www.alcoholics-anonymous.org

Alcoholics Anonymous is a fellowship of men and women who share their experience, strength, and hope with one another so that they may solve their common problem and help others to recover from alcoholism while applying the twelve steps, twelve traditions, and twelve concepts of service.

Al-Anon Family Group Headquarters Inc.
1600 Corporate Landing Parkway
Virginia Beach, Virginia 23454-5617
Phone: (757)-563-1600
Fax: (757)-563-1655
www.al-anon.alateen.org
Email: WSO@al-anon.org

Al-Anon's program of recovery is based on the twelve steps, twelve traditions, and twelve concepts of service adapted from Alcoholics Anonymous (AA). Includes Al-Anon Family and Alateen information.

Adult Children of Alcoholics World Service Organization
Post Office Box 3216
Torrance, California 90510
(310)534-1815
www.adultchildren.org

Created to serve the fellowship of Adult Children of Alcoholics by sharing information and experiences with one another and by applying the twelve steps upon which Alcoholics Anonymous is founded.

Codependent Anonymous
Post Office Box 33577
Phoenix, Arizona 85067
Phone: (602) 277-7991
www.codependents.org

Codependents Anonymous is fellowship whose common purpose is to develop healthy relationships through applying the twelve steps and principles of CoDA to daily life.

Narcotics Anonymous
World Service Office
Post Office Box 9999
Van Nuys, California 91409
Phone: (818) 773-9999
Fax: (818) 700-0700
www.na.org
Email: info@na.org

Narcotics Anonymous is an international community-based association of recovering drug addicts.

National Council on Alcoholism and Drug Dependence
20 Exchange Place
New York, New York 10005
Phone: (212) 269-7797
Twenty-four-hour affiliate referral line: (800) NCA-CALL
www.ncadd.org

Provides education, information, help, and hope to the public for the purpose of dealing with drug dependence.

Cocaine Anonymous World Service Organization
Post Office Box 2000
Los Angeles, California 90049
(800)347-8998
www.ca.org

Cocaine Anonymous is a fellowship of men and women who share their strength and hope with one another so that they may solve their common problem and help others to recover from their addiction.

Anorexia Nervosa & Associated (Eating) Disorders
Post Office Box 7
Highland Park, Illinois 60035
Phone: (847) 831-3438
www.anad.org

A nonprofit corporation seeking to alleviate the problems of eating disorders, to educate the general public and professionals in the health-care field, and to encourage and provide research to discover the causes of eating disorders, methods of prevention, types of treatments and their effectiveness.

Overeaters Anonymous World Services Office
Post Office Box 44020
Rio Rancho, New Mexico 87174
Phone: (505) 891-2664
www.oa.org

OA offers a program of recovery from compulsive overeating using the twelve steps and twelve traditions of AA. OA is not just about weight loss, obesity, or diets. It addresses physical emotional and spiritual well-being.

Sex Addicts Anonymous
Post Office Box 70949
Houston, Texas 77270
Phone: (800) 477-8191
www.sexaa.org

A spiritual program based on the principles and traditions of Alcoholics Anonymous.

Marijuana Anonymous World Service
Post Office Box 2912
Van Nuys, California 91404
Phone: (800)766-6779
www.marijuana-anonymous.org

MA uses the basic twelve steps of recovery found by Alcoholics Anonymous to recover from the marijuana addiction.

Author
Art Gilles

ABOUT THE AUTHOR

**Sobriety Castle
The Fall and Rise
of Stuart MacPherson
A novel by Art Gilles
"Alcoholism is a lonely demon."**

Steven F: Art Gilles is an honorably discharged United States Navy veteran and a recovered alcoholic and drug addict who maintains continued and progressive recovery through a lifestyle of helping others. Sobriety date is April 1992.

Art earned a certificate of alcohol and drug studies and an associate of arts degree in human services. Art graduated Cal State University with honors, obtaining a bachelor of arts degree in psychology and a master of art degree in counseling.

Art is a writer, artist, singer, songwriter, and guitar player.

Alex: Art Gilles's many enriching and exciting life experiences make for good writing and show up in this tremendously exciting novel.

Allison: The author changed and saved my life by doing an intervention on me and brought me to a twelve-step meeting. I believed I would have died from alcohol and drug use if he did not come then.

CPSIA information can be obtained
at www.ICGtesting.com
Printed in the USA
BVHW061809180422
634310BV00001B/1